The New World Haggadah

הגדת העולם החדש

The New World Haggadah

הגדת העולם החדש

Ilan Stavans

Art by

Gloria Abella Ballen

Introduction

Ilan Stavans

THE PROMISE OF FREEDOM IS THE ENGINE OF HUMAN PROGRESS. People seek it at every turn, at any cost, no matter what.

This makes the Passover story endlessly resonant. The biblical Moses is a greater than life mythical figure. The depiction we get of him is of an imperfect, reluctant leader who kills an Egyptian in his youth and runs away soon after, who is miserable at public speaking and suffers from an irate temperament, and who, more than anything, is ambivalent about his relationship with the Divine. Yet, in spite of himself, he frees the Israelites from slavery, guides them out of Egypt, and takes them through an odyssey in the desert that tests them at every turn and ultimately defines them as a nation. No wonder the heroic achievement of Moses and the Israelites has been celebrated in song and story throughout history.

I remember with affection the Passover dinners in my native Mexico. My ancestors were immigrants from Poland and other parts of the "Pale of Settlement." They had arrived at the dawn of the twentieth century, settling in a mestizo country deeply rooted in the Catholic faith and radically different from the place they had left behind. They crossed the Atlantic escaping poverty and anti-Semitic persecution because they wanted a chance to prosper and to practice their religion without fear. In the Seder, Moisés, as he is known in Spanish, was a lionhearted leader compared to Christopher Columbus, to Ernesto Ché Guevara, to Nelson Mandela.

We were a large number of relatives who would congregate around a table for almost four hours, eating food from the Old Country and delicious Mexican dishes. On occasion we would have Sephardic foods as well. Adults would drink four cups of wine, each representing an aspect of the inner and outer journey of the Jews. At the center of the table we had a plentiful supply of unleavened bread, matzah, which I liked to spread with *cajeta*, a soft caramel paste special to Mexico. There were pillows all around for sitting, and as children we loved pillow fighting before the Seder began.

On the Seder plate we had matzah, *maror* (bitter herbs), symbolizing the harshness of slavery; *charoset* (the mix of chopped nuts, grated apples, cinnamon, and sweet red wine), representing the mortar used by the Jews to build the storage cities of Pithom and Raamses; *karpas* (a vegetable dipped in salt water); *z'roa* (a shank bone, usually from lamb or goat), to remember the destruction of the temple in Jerusalem; and *beitzah* (boiled egg), as a springtime motif.

The adults told us that another guest, *Profeta Elías*, could arrive at anytime. The door would be open for him, and there would be an empty seat at the table with a wineglass filled to the brim. A portion of the matzah, shown to all by the leader of the Seder, became the *afikoman*, from Greek for afterwards, and it was eaten at the end of the meal. The *afikoman* was hidden for the young to look for when the proper time arrived. Whoever found it was awarded ten pesos and a *trompo*, a Mexican top.

The storytelling was filled with references to the Holocaust, where a part of our family had perished and references to Zionism as the dream of the homeland that could bring us back to Israel, as Moses had once done.

Our daily life in Mexico had an important presence in the Passover story. There were anecdotes about *la convivencia*, when, between the ninth and the fifteenth centuries, Jews, Muslims, and Christians coexisted in the Iberian Peninsula. And about the plight of the *conversos* and crypto-Jews escaping the Holy Office of the Inquisition. Likewise, indigenous tales were told. And children heard about Cuauthémoc, the last Aztec emperor, who resisted the merciless soldiers of Hernán Cortés. And about Father Miguel Hidalgo y Costilla and José María Morelos y Pavón, who led the Mexican movement for independence in 1810. I remember being enthralled by the richness and variety of these stories.

Then, in my mid-twenties, I became an immigrant to the United States, leaving Mexico because it wasn't open and democratic, and I didn't feel I could explore ideas in public, fully and without intimidation. I wanted to live in a free country, but the odyssey wasn't easy. My English was precarious, and I constantly felt like an outsider.

By happenstance, my first Passover in this country, which was in New York at the house of a rabbi-in-training, was one of the earliest moments when I felt at home here. In this Sephardic Passover ritual, I heard an African-American spiritual, "Go Down Moses." It was totally new to me, and I was asked if I could say a few words about the *desaparecidos* in Argentina's Dirty War and their struggle against oppression, which I related with my limited vocabulary.

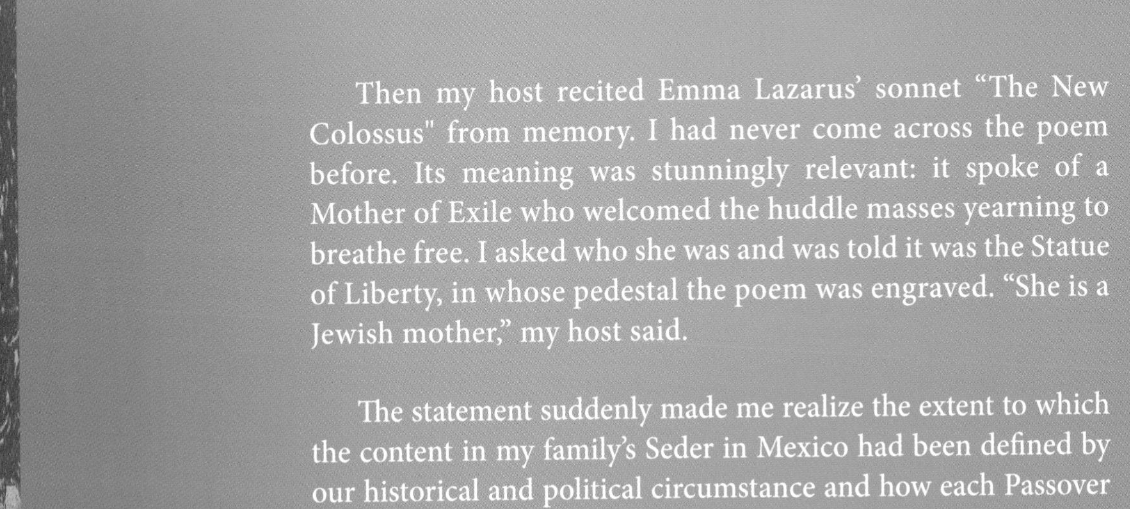

Then my host recited Emma Lazarus' sonnet "The New Colossus" from memory. I had never come across the poem before. Its meaning was stunningly relevant: it spoke of a Mother of Exile who welcomed the huddle masses yearning to breathe free. I asked who she was and was told it was the Statue of Liberty, in whose pedestal the poem was engraved. "She is a Jewish mother," my host said.

The statement suddenly made me realize the extent to which the content in my family's Seder in Mexico had been defined by our historical and political circumstance and how each Passover is experienced in its own unique way by its participants. I mentioned this to my host, who answered: "Yes, each of us adds to that difference."

My intention in *The New World Haggadah* is to make Moses emblematic of today's complex world. Not too long ago, I discovered another poem by Emma Lazarus that in my eyes is quite similar to "The New Colossus." It is called "1492" and it looks at that *annus mirabilis* as a fracturing moment, a kind of Big Bang that gave birth to a cornucopia of Diaspora events, each with its own metabolism.

The Jewish Diaspora across the Mediterranean Basin, the Middle East, and the Atlantic Ocean to what we call the Americas is exemplified by a plethora of languages and traditions. I want to bridge the gap between North and South and between East and West, between Ashkenazim and Sephardim, and between Africans, Europeans, and mestizos. 1492 is the year that changed the world. For better or worse we were all born from the common wellspring of those events.

What makes this a new Haggadah is its multicultural—and multilingual—qualities, like growing up Jewish and speaking Yiddish in Catholic, Spanish-speaking Mexico. Even today, sitting at the Seder table looking at the matzah, *maror*, and other ubiquitous culinary ingredients, my mouth still salivates thinking about the *cajeta* in our Seders in Mexico.

I have reconfigured the liturgy to be more embracing, inserting voices seeking freedom through renewal. Among others are the Ladino cumulative song *Un Cavritico*, a chant used during the Civil Rights Movement, a protest song, a traditional Judeo-Spanish song about Moses leaving Egypt, and a disquisition about having one's heart divided by the medieval poet Yehuda Halevi. The gorgeous art of Gloria Abella Ballen enlivens every page.

Like Moses, each of us is a symbol because others see themselves reflected in us. Others live their lives through ours. To me, Passover is about realizing that we are at once imprisoned in our moment in time and space and simultaneously free to wander to other times and places through the power of our imagination. This Passover story transports us to a time long ago when great men and women and great events led a people to freedom.

The story of Exodus is a human story. It is universal. My dream is that the diversity in this narrative will make all of us feel that it is ours. The act of repeating the Exodus story is liberating and gaining freedom is a continuous process. We might not be fully free, but each of us is in the process of breaking from our slavery, our "Egypt".

THE PROMISE OF FREEDOM KEEPS US ALIVE...

Mitzrayim

Seder-Night

Israel Zangwill (1864–1926)

British author and founding Zionist thinker who befriended Theodor Herzl. He was one of the first to mention the idea of the American Melting Pot. One of his characters says, "America is God's Crucible, the great Melting-Pot where all the races of Europe are melting and reforming."

Prosaic miles of streets stretch all round,
Astir with restless, hurried life and spanned
By arches that with thund'rous trains resound,
And throbbing wires that galvanize the land;
Gin-palaces in tawdry splendor stand;
The newsboys shriek of mangled bodies found;
The last burlesque is playing in the Strand—
In modern prose all poetry seems drowned.
Yet in ten thousand homes this April night
An ancient People celebrates its birth
To Freedom, with a reverential mirth,
With customs quaint and many a hoary rite,
Waiting until, its tarnished glories bright,
Its God shall be the God of all the earth.

גלות

Emma Lazarus (1849-1887)

Born New York City,
Sephardic American poet.

These two sonnets, arguably among the most famous in Jewish culture, establish a connection between the Edict of Expulsion of the Jews from Spain and their arrival to the United States as a safe-haven centuries later.

1492

Thou two-faced year, Mother of Change and Fate,
Didst weep when Spain cast forth with flaming sword,
The children of the prophets of the Lord,
Prince, priest, and people, spurned by zealot hate.

Hounded from sea to sea, from state to state,
The West refused them, and the East abhorred.
No anchorage the known world could afford,
Close-locked was every port, barred every gate.

Then smiling, thou unveil'dst, O two-faced year,
A virgin world where doors of sunset part,
Saying, "Ho, all who weary, enter here!

There falls each ancient barrier that the art
Of race or creed or rank devised, to rear
Grim bulwarked hatred between heart and heart!"

The New Colossus

Not like the brazen giant of Greek fame,
With conquering limbs astride from land to land;
Here at our sea-washed, sunset gates shall stand
A mighty woman with a torch, whose flame

Is the imprisoned lightning, and her name
Mother of Exiles. From her beacon-hand
Glows world-wide welcome; her mild eyes command
The air-bridged harbor that twin cities frame.

"Keep, ancient lands, your storied pomp!" cries she
With silent lips. "Give me your tired, your poor,
Your huddled masses yearning to breathe free,

The wretched refuse of your teeming shore.
Send these, the homeless, tempest-tost to me,
I lift my lamp beside the golden door!"

The Kiddush

Pour the first cup of wine.
Holding the wine, the head of the table reads.

Shema Israel

Ilan Stavans

We are made of letters
that turn to words,
sentences,
paragraphs
and a book—
the Book of Books.
Through it
we sing your praise.
We have nothing else—
these letters,
these words,
this book is home.

Shema Israel:
In granting us language,
you make us whole.
In narrating us, we find purpose.
You are our scribe,
we are your characters.
We are your story,
you live in ours.

Shema Israel,
Adonai Eloheinu,
Adonai Echad.

לתורה

The head of the table points to the Seder plate, naming the following foods and asking a participant to explain the symbolism of each:

- *Matzah* (unleavened bread)
- *Maror* (bitter herbs)
- *Charoset* (fruit and nut mix with red wine)
- *Karpas* (vegetable dipped in salt water)
- *Z'roa* (a shank bone from a lamb or goat)
- *Beitzah* (boiled egg).

The head of the table explains the cup for the Prophet Elijah and the *afikoman* (the portion of *matzah* to be hidden from the children) and makes sure everyone has pillows to recline.

Happiness

Ilan Stavans

I've lived long enough
to know
that happiness
never comes on its own,
unadvertised,
by accident;
it needs to be wanted,
it needs to be found.

Five things
make me happy.
The first one is friendship.
My lover,
my offspring,
my parents
and siblings,
and,
of course,
my friends.
They all are the yardstick
by which I measure
everything
and by which I should
be measured.
Their sadness is my sadness.
Their pleasure is my pleasure.

The second thing
that makes me happy
is shelter.
I love my house—the many
houses I've had:
their structure,
warmth,
aroma,
the person I was in them.
Every crevice,
every speck of dust
is mapped
in my body.
Without my houses
I would be bodiless.

The third thing is food and wine.
I savor
the taste
of corn,
of pepper,
and chocolate
the taste of aged cheese,
olives,
and watermelon;
I savor
a cup of herbal tea
and carrot cake
and a plum.
I would be tasteless
without these flavors.
How can I
begin to thank
the earth
for its generosity,
for its diversity,
for its sustenance?

The fourth is peace.
When I'm angry,
when I'm in turmoil,
when I'm upset,
my inner world is in disarray,
I'm trapped in chaos.
I need serenity,
I need calmness.

And the fifth and last thing
—you won't be surprised—
is intimately linked
to all previous ones:
I need clarity.
Thinking plainly,
thinking honestly,
compassionately,
unapologetically,
with equanimity,
thinking on my own,
following my train of thought
as it traverses
the unending ocean
of ideas
that is life,
pondering
what's good
and what isn't,
fills me with joy.

Every day
I remind myself
that I'm a rational being
and that
the capacity to be happy is,
first and foremost,
about balance.

I could list other things
(many other),
like music, for instance,
or reading Neruda's odes,
but why?
This list,
the conviction
it grants me
—knowing what I have,
having what I know—
is all I need
to be happy.

Angelina Muñiz-Huberman

(Born 1936)

Born in France to parents escaping the Spanish Civil War, Mexican novelist, poet, and scholar devoted to Sephardic culture.

Pesaj
(Spanish/English)

En medio del recuerdo me perdí en una luz
sin saber de qué estrella era.

Abrí la ventana y el olor del aire
trepó por los muros como una polilla.

Las velas encendidas se apagaron
y el vino derramado cubrió el mantel.

La luna brilló entre las sábanas blancas
para que la noche de amor se iluminara.

Alguien cruzó el mar y todos lo siguieron
a la espera de un inmenso desierto de libertad.

Piedras y arena marcaron el camino
cánticos y una danza de velos y eternidad.

Los niños enmarcaron su memoria
con cuatro preguntas una sola vez labradas.

A las doce de la noche el búho voló
y la puerta entreabierta fue la bendición.

Viajeros de toda tierra
al fin descansan.

Passover

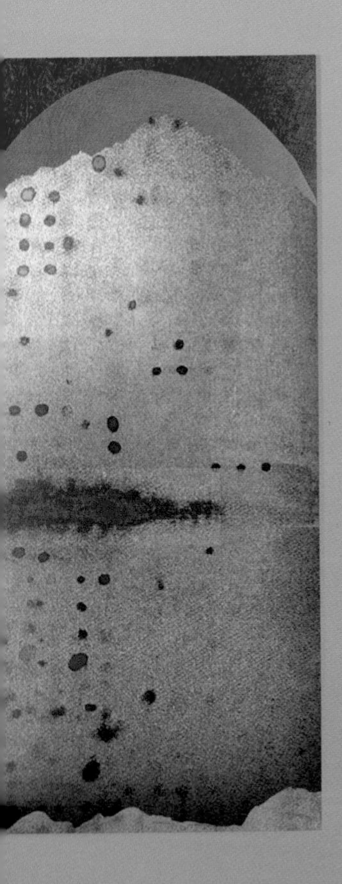

Immersed in memory, I lost myself in a light,
What star it came from, I could not say.

I opened the window and the scent of air
Climbed, like a moth, over the walls.

The lit candles were blown out
And the spilt wine covered the tablecloth.

The moon shone on the white linen,
Illuminating the night of love.

One crossed the sea and all followed,
Awaiting an immense desert of liberty.

Stone and sand marked the way,
Songs and a dance of veils, and eternity.

Children framed their memory
With four questions only once engraved.

At midnight the owl spread its wings
And the half-opened door became a blessing.

Travelers of all lands
may you rest at last.

If it is Sabbath, recite this verse about creation.

וַיְהִי-עֶרֶב וַיְהִי-בֹקֶר יוֹם הַשִּׁשִּׁי.
וַיְכֻלּוּ הַשָּׁמַיִם וְהָאָרֶץ וְכָל-צְבָאָם:
וַיְכַל אֱלֹהִים בַּיּוֹם הַשְּׁבִיעִי מְלַאכְתּוֹ
אֲשֶׁר עָשָׂה. וַיִּשְׁבֹּת בַּיּוֹם הַשְּׁבִיעִי
מִכָּל-מְלַאכְתּוֹ אֲשֶׁר עָשָׂה. וַיְבָרֶךְ
אֱלֹהִים אֶת-יוֹם הַשְּׁבִיעִי וַיְקַדֵּשׁ אֹתוֹ
כִּי בוֹ שָׁבַת מִכָּל-מְלַאכְתּוֹ אֲשֶׁר בָּרָא
אֱלֹהִים לַעֲשׂוֹת:

And there was evening and there was morning, the sixth day. And the heaven and the earth were finished, and all the host of them. And on the seventh day God wrapped up the work done; and God rested on the seventh day from all the work done. And God blessed the seventh day, and hallowed it; because that in it God rested from all the work done which God had created.

Every Jewish ceremony begins with a blessing, and these blessings have existed for generations.

Start with these blessings.

בָּרוּךְ אַתָּה יְיָ אֱלֹהֵינוּ מֶלֶךְ הָעוֹלָם בּוֹרֵא פְּרִי הַגָּפֶן

Blessed are You, our God, creator of the fruit of the vine.

continue

בָּרוּךְ אַתָּה יְיָ אֱלֹהֵינוּ מֶלֶךְ הָעוֹלָם. אֲשֶׁר בָּחַר בָּנוּ מִכָּל-עָם. וְרוֹ-
מְמָנוּ מִכָּל-לָשׁוֹן. וְקִדְּשָׁנוּ בְּמִצְוֹתָיו. וַתִּתֶּן-לָנוּ יְיָ אֱלֹהֵינוּ בְּאַהֲבָה
[שַׁבָּתוֹת לִמְנוּחָה וּ] מוֹעֲדִים לְשִׂמְחָה. חַגִּים וּזְמַנִּים לְשָׂשׂוֹן. אֶת-יוֹם
[הַשַּׁבָּת הַזֶּה וְאֶת-יוֹם] חַג הַמַּצּוֹת הַזֶּה זְמַן חֵרוּתֵנוּ [בְּאַהֲבָה] מִקְרָא-
קֹדֶשׁ זֵכֶר לִיצִיאַת מִצְרָיִם. כִּי בָנוּ בָחַרְתָּ וְאוֹתָנוּ קִדַּשְׁתָּ מִכָּל-הָעַמִּים
[וְשַׁבָּת] וּמוֹעֲדֵי קָדְשֶׁךָ [בְּאַהֲבָה וּבְרָצוֹן] בְּשִׂמְחָה וּבְשָׂשׂוֹן הִנְחַלְתָּנוּ.
בָּרוּךְ אַתָּה יְיָ מְקַדֵּשׁ [הַשַּׁבָּת וְ] יִשְׂרָאֵל וְהַזְּמַנִּים.

BLESSED are You, our God, master of the universe, who chose us from every people, and exalted us among every tongue, and sanctified us by your commandments. With love have you given us, our God, holidays for gladness, [Sabbaths for rest] festivals and seasons for rejoicing, this [Sabbath day and this] day of the festival of unleavened bread, the season of our deliverance, [with love] a holy convocation in remembrance of the departure from Egypt. You have chosen us, and we are sanctified from all other peoples. [And the Sabbath] And the holidays of thy sanctification [with love and favor] hast thou given us, with gladness and joy to inherit. Blessed are You, God, who sanctifies [the Sabbath and] Israel and the seasons.

RECITE THESE BLESSINGS IF THE SEDER IS AT THE CLOSE OF SABBATH.

בָּרוּךְ אַתָּה יְיָ אֱלֹהֵינוּ מֶלֶךְ הָעוֹלָם, בּוֹרֵא מְאוֹרֵי הָאֵשׁ:

בָּרוּךְ אַתָּה יְיָ אֱלֹהֵינוּ מֶלֶךְ הָעוֹלָם, הַמַּבְדִּיל בֵּין קֹדֶשׁ לְחוֹל. בֵּין אוֹר לְחשֶׁךְ, בֵּין יִשְׂרָאֵל לָעַמִּים, בֵּין יוֹם הַשְּׁבִיעִי לְשֵׁשֶׁת יְמֵי הַמַּ־עֲשֶׂה. בֵּין קְדֻשַּׁת שַׁבָּת לִקְדֻשַּׁת יוֹם טוֹב הִבְדַּלְתָּ. וְאֶת-יוֹם הַשְּׁבִי־עִי מִשֵּׁשֶׁת יְמֵי-הַמַּעֲשֶׂה קִדַּשְׁתָּ. הִבְדַּלְתָּ וְקִדַּשְׁתָּ אֶת-עַמְּךָ יִשְׂרָאֵל בִּקְדֻשָּׁתֶךָ. בָּרוּךְ אַתָּה יְיָ, הַמַּבְדִּיל בֵּין קֹדֶשׁ לְקֹדֶשׁ:

בָּרוּךְ אַתָּה יְיָ אֱלֹהֵינוּ מֶלֶךְ הָעוֹלָם שֶׁהֶחֱיָנוּ וְקִיְּמָנוּ וְהִגִּיעָנוּ לַזְּמַן הַזֶּה:

Blessed are You, our God, master of the universe, creator of the light of the fire.

Blessed are You, our God, master of the universe, who divides the holy from the profane, light from darkness, Israel from the nations, the seventh day from the six days of work; the sanctity of the Sabbath from the sanctity of the holiday have you divided, and have sanctified the seventh day above the six days of work. You have set apart and hallowed your people Israel with your sanctity. Blessed are You, God, who divides sanctity from sanctity.

Blessed are You, our God, master of the universe, who has kept us alive, and sustained us, and enabled us to reach this season.

The first cup of wine is drunk in a reclining position.

MIGUEL LEVÍ DE BARRIOS

(1625–1701)

Born in Spain (aka Daniel ha-Levi),
Spanish *converso* poet and historian who returned to Judaism. Died in Amsterdam.

EL PRIMER HOMBRE

(Spanish/English)

El primer hombre fui, que, por Dios hecho,
le semejé, de todo cifra hermosa;
y, con ingratitud al cielo odiosa,
el quererme hacer grande me ha deshecho.

Dominé el mundo, a mi altivez estrecho,
y por comer la fruta venenosa,
de la muerte en la cárcel espantosa,
me viene grande el más pequeño trecho.

Denominéme, de adamá (que 'tierra'
denota), Adán (que es 'hombre') por tal modo
que he vuelto a mi materia inanimada.

Lo que esta losa hasta mi nombre encierra,
cuando Adán fue pensaba que era todo
y, leído al contrario, ya soy nada.

The First Man

I was the first man, by God handmade,
I appeared to be, by every standard handsome;
And, with ingratitude to the hateful heavens,
The desire to make myself grand has destroyed me.

I dominated the world, with my rigid pride,
And by consuming the poisonous fruit,
By the death in the petrifying prison,
The smallest space has become too large for me.

Named, by a woman (which 'land' denotes),
Adam (which is 'man') by these means
I have returned to my inanimate state.

What this thin slab encloses, even my name,
When Adam was, he thought he was everything
And, learning the contrary, I am now nothing.

Translation Rebecca Pol and Ilan Stavans

Washing of Hands

וּרְחַץ

A pitcher, basin, and towel are offered to those present to wash their hands. The head of the table dips some celery or other vegetable in salt water (or vinegar) and then offers *karpas* (a piece of the vegetable) to each person.

כַּרְפַּס

Say the following blessing before eating the *karpas*.

בָּרוּךְ אַתָּה יְיָ אֱלֹהֵינוּ מֶלֶךְ הָעוֹלָם בּוֹרֵא פְּרִי הָאֲדָמָה

Blessed are You, our God, master of the universe, who creates the fruit of the earth.

Continue with the following.

Yehuda Halevi

(1075 — 1141)

Born in Spain. Poet, physician, and philosopher who died on his way to Palestine.

לִבִּי בְמִזְרָח

(Hebrew/English)

לִבִּי בְמִזְרָח, וְאָנֹכִי בְּסוֹף מַעֲרָב
אֵיךְ אֶטְעֲמָה אֵת אֲשֶׁר אֹכַל וְאֵיךְ יֶעֱרָב
אֵיכָה אֲשַׁלֵּם נְדָרַי וֶאֱסָרַי, בְּעוֹד
צִיּוֹן בְּחֶבֶל אֱדוֹם וַאֲנִי בְּכֶבֶל עֲרָב
יֵקַל בְּעֵינַי עֲזֹב כָּל טוּב סְפָרַד, כְּמוֹ
יֵקַר בְּעֵינַי רְאוֹת עַפְרוֹת דְּבִיר נֶחֱרָב.

A Heart Divided

My heart is in the East and I am at the edge of the West.
How should I taste what I eat and how to enjoy it?
How should I fulfill my vows and pledges
while Zion is under Edom and I am in the Arabian confines?
It would be simple in my eyes to leave behind Spain's joys,
like looking at the heavenly dust of the ruined shrine.

—Translation Ilan Stavans

Isaac Aboab da Fonseca

(1605-1693)

Born in Portugal to a *converso* family. Migrated to Amsterdam and returned to Judaism.
First rabbi in the Americas in Recife, Brazil.
Written in 1646, this is the first Hebrew writing from the Americas.

מי כמוך

(Hebrew/English)

מי כמוך ואין כמוך   מי דומה לך ואין דומה לך

אל אלהימ אדני   רם על כל רמים שוכן מעוני

שמו אזכיר בקהל אמוני   בזמירות נריע לו

בפשעי השלכתי לארץ מרחקים   ודברי נביאיו כי הקים

ואם נפלתי משחקים לעמקים   אשרי אדם עוז לו

גלי הים עברו על ראשי   ואף גם זאת נכספה נפשו

ולא שקרתי בקדושי   ובריתי נאמנת לו

דבקה רוחי אחריו   אשורי לא נטו מאשוריו

נפשי יצחק בדבוריו   על כן אוחיל לו

הזכירו כי נשגב שמו   ולא העיר כל זעמו

וירם קרן לעמו   העמ בחר לנחלה לו

Who is Like You?

Who is like You? There is none like You.
Who resembles You? None resembles You.
Great God, the Lord,
Exalted above all, dwelling in my abode.
I shall invoke His name in the assembly of the faithful,
We shall acclaim Him with songs of praise.
Due to my sins, I was cast off to a far-away land,
thus fulfilling the words of His prophets to me.
But even if I have fallen from the heights to the depths,
Happy is the man for whom God is his refuge.
Ocean waves passed over my head,
And even still my soul longed for Him.
I have not been false to my Holy One,
My covenant is faithful to Him.
My spirit has clung to Him,
My steps have not deviated from His steps.
My soul rejoices in His words,
Therefore I will hope in Him.
Declare that His name is exalted,
He has not given full vent to His fury.
He has raised up the horn of His people,
the people whom He has chosen for His possession.

— Translation David Gilad and Orit Rabkin

Bread of Affliction

יַחַץ

The head of the table takes the middle one of the three pieces of matzah on the Seder plate, breaks it into two parts and wraps the larger half in a cloth and sets it aside for the *afikoman*. Sometime soon the *afikoman* will disappear from the table to be hidden somewhere in the house by the head of the table, without anyone watching.

The head of the table removes the *z'roa* (shank bone) and the egg from the Seder plate. Those sitting nearby lift up the Seder plate. Everyone recites the blessing.

הָא לַחְמָא עַנְיָא דִי-אֲכָלוּ אַבְהָתָנָא בְּאַרְעָא דְמִצְרָיִם. כָּל דִכְפִין יֵיתֵי וְיֵכֻל, כָּל-דִצְרִיךְ יֵיתֵי וְיִפְסַח. הַשַּׁתָּא הָכָא, לְשָׁנָה הַבָּאָה בְּאַרְעָא דְיִשְׂרָאֵל. הַשַּׁתָּא עַבְדֵי, לְשָׁנָה הַבָּאָה בְּנֵי חוֹרִין:

This is the bread of poverty which our forefathers and foremothers ate in the land of Egypt. Let all who are hungry enter and eat; let all who are needy come to our Passover feast. This year we are here; next year may we be in the Land of Israel. This year we are slaves; next year may we be free men.

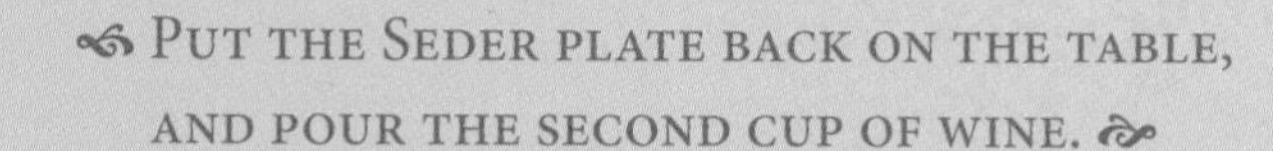
Put the Seder plate back on the table, and pour the second cup of wine.

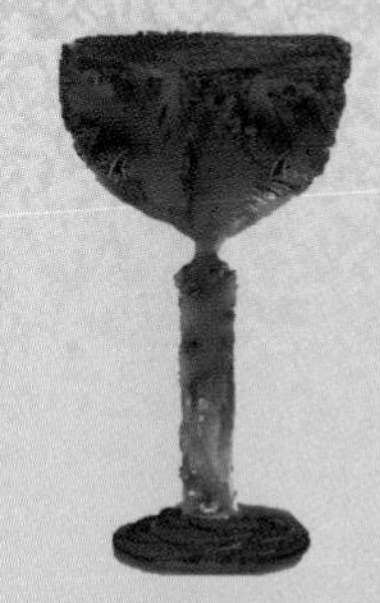

הָא לַחְמָא עַנְיָא

The Four Questions

The youngest person at the Seder asks the following four questions.

מַה נִּשְׁתַּנָּה הַלַּיְלָה הַזֶּה מִכָּל הַלֵּילוֹת:

א שֶׁבְּכָל הַלֵּילוֹת אָנוּ אוֹכְלִין חָמֵץ וּמַצָּה. הַלַּיְלָה הַזֶּה כֻּלּוֹ מַצָּה:

ב שֶׁבְּכָל הַלֵּילוֹת אָנוּ אוֹכְלִין שְׁאָר יְרָקוֹת הַלַּיְלָה הַזֶּה מָרוֹר:

ג שֶׁבְּכָל הַלֵּילוֹת אֵין אָנוּ מַטְבִּילִין אֲפִילוּ פַּעַם אֶחָת.
הַלַּיְלָה הַזֶּה שְׁתֵּי פְעָמִים:

ד שֶׁבְּכָל הַלֵּילוֹת אָנוּ אוֹכְלִין בֵּין יוֹשְׁבִין וּבֵין מְסֻבִּין.
הַלַּיְלָה הַזֶּה כֻּלָּנוּ מְסֻבִּין:

Why does this night differ from all other nights? For on all other nights we eat either leavened or unleavened bread; why on this night only unleavened bread?

On all other nights we eat all kinds of herbs; why on this night only bitter herbs?

On all other nights we need not dip our herbs even once; why on this night must we dip them twice?

On all other nights we eat either sitting up or reclining; why on this night do we all recline?

Ma Nishtana

(The Four Questions)

Transliteration

Ma Nishtana ha laila ha-ze mikol haleilot. Mikol haleilot.

Sheb'chol haleilot, anu ochlin, chametz u'matzah, chametz u'matzah.

Halaila haze, halaila haze, kulo matzah

Halaila haze, halaila haze, kulo matzah

Sheb'chol haleilot anu ochlin she'ar irakot, she'ar irakot.

Halaila haze, halaila haze maror, maror.

She b'chol haleilot ein anu matbilin, afilu pa'am achat, afilu pa'am achat.

Halaila haze, halaila haze, shtei pe'amin

Halaila haze, halaila haze, shtei pe'amin

She b'chol haleilot anu ochlin, bein yoshvin uvein mesubin, bein yoshvin uvein mesubin.

Halailah haze, halaila haze, kulanu mesubin

Halailah haze, halaila haze, kulanu mesubin

The head of the table recites the reply with all the celebrants.

עֲבָדִים הָיִינוּ לְפַרְעֹה בְּמִצְרָיִם. וַיּוֹצִיאֵנוּ יְיָ אֱלֹהֵינוּ מִשָּׁם, בְּיָד
חֲזָקָה וּבִזְרֹעַ נְטוּיָה, וְאִלּוּ לֹא הוֹצִיא הַקָּדוֹשׁ בָּרוּךְ הוּא אֶת
אֲבוֹתֵינוּ מִמִּצְרַיִם, הֲרֵי אָנוּ וּבָנֵינוּ וּבְנֵי בָנֵינוּ, מְשֻׁעְבָּדִים הָיִינוּ
לְפַרְעֹה בְּמִצְרָיִם. וַאֲפִילוּ כֻּלָּנוּ חֲכָמִים כֻּלָּנוּ נְבוֹנִים, כֻּלָּנוּ זְקֵ־
נִים, כֻּלָּנוּ יוֹדְעִים אֶת-הַתּוֹרָה, מִצְוָה עָלֵינוּ לְסַפֵּר בִּיצִיאַת מִצְ־
רַיִם. וְכָל-הַמַּרְבֶּה לְסַפֵּר בִּיצִיאַת מִצְרַיִם, הֲרֵי זֶה מְשֻׁבָּח:
מַעֲשֶׂה בְּרַבִּי אֱלִיעֶזֶר, וְרַבִּי יְהוֹשֻׁעַ, וְרַבִּי אֶלְעָזָר בֶּן-עֲזַרְיָה
וְרַבִּי עֲקִיבָא וְרַבִּי טַרְפוֹן שֶׁהָיוּ מְסֻבִּין בִּבְנֵי בְרַק, וְהָיוּ מְסַפְּ־
רִים בִּיצִיאַת מִצְרַיִם כָּל-אוֹתוֹ הַלַּיְלָה, עַד-שֶׁבָּאוּ תַלְמִידֵיהֶם
וְאָמְרוּ לָהֶם. רַבּוֹתֵינוּ, הִגִּיעַ זְמַן קְרִיאַת שְׁמַע שֶׁל-שַׁחֲרִית:
אָמַר רַבִּי אֶלְעָזָר בֶּן-עֲזַרְיָה. הֲרֵי אֲנִי כְּבֶן-שִׁבְעִים שָׁנָה, וְלֹא
זָכִיתִי שֶׁתֵּאָמֵר יְצִיאַת מִצְרַיִם בַּלֵּילוֹת. עַד שֶׁדְּרָשָׁהּ בֶּן-
זוֹמָא. שֶׁנֶּאֱמַר: לְמַעַן תִּזְכֹּר אֶת יוֹם צֵאתְךָ מֵאֶרֶץ מִצְרַיִם כֹּל
יְמֵי חַיֶּיךָ: יְמֵי חַיֶּיךָ הַיָּמִים. כֹּל יְמֵי חַיֶּיךָ הַלֵּילוֹת. וַחֲכָמִים
אוֹמְרִים יְמֵי חַיֶּיךָ הָעוֹלָם הַזֶּה. כֹּל יְמֵי חַיֶּיךָ לְהָבִיא לִימוֹת
הַמָּשִׁיחַ:

We were Pharaoh's slaves in Egypt, and God brought us forth from there with a mighty hand and an outstretched arm. And if God had not brought our ancestors forth from Egypt, then we, our children, and our children's children, would still be Pharaoh's slaves.

So, even if all of us were wise, all of us full of understanding, all of us elders, all of us knowing in Torah, we should still be under the commandment to tell the story of the departure from Egypt. And the more one tells the story of the departure from Egypt, the more praiseworthy it becomes.

A tale is told of Rabbi Eliezer, Rabbi Joshua, Rabbi Eleazar ben Azariah, Rabbi Akiba, and Rabbi Tarfon, who once reclined together at Bene Berak, telling about the departure from Egypt all night, until their disciples came to them and said, "Masters, the time has come to say the morning *shema*."

Rabbi Eleazar ben Azariah said: "I feel like a man of seventy years, yet I never understood why the story concerning the departure from Egypt should be recited at night, until Ben Zoma interpreted it so. So it is said [Deuteronomy. 16:3]: "That you may remember the day when you came forth out of the land of Egypt all the days of your life." Had it been written 'the days of your life,' it would have meant the days only; but 'all the days of your life' means the nights as well."

הוּא אוֹמֵר

בָּרוּךְ הַמָּקוֹם. בָּרוּךְ הוּא. בָּרוּךְ שֶׁנָּתַן תּוֹרָה לְעַמּוֹ יִשְׂרָאֵל. בָּרוּךְ הוּא. כְּנֶגֶד אַרְבָּעָה בָנִים דִּבְּרָה תוֹרָה. אֶחָד חָכָם, וְאֶחָד רָשָׁע, וְאֶחָד תָּם. וְאֶחָד שֶׁאֵינוֹ יוֹדֵעַ לִשְׁאוֹל:

חָכָם מַה הוּא אוֹמֵר. מָה הָעֵדֹת וְהַחֻקִּים וְהַמִּשְׁפָּטִים, אֲשֶׁר צִוָּה יְיָ אֱלֹהֵינוּ אֶתְכֶם: וְאַף אַתָּה אֱמָר לוֹ כְּהִלְכוֹת הַפֶּסַח. אֵין מַפְטִירִין אַחַר הַפֶּסַח אֲפִיקוֹמָן:

רָשָׁע מַה הוּא אוֹמֵר. מָה הָעֲבוֹדָה הַזֹּאת לָכֶם: לָכֶם וְלֹא לוֹ. וּלְפִי שֶׁהוֹצִיא אֶת-עַצְמוֹ מִן-הַכְּלָל, כָּפַר בָּעִקָּר. וְאַף אַתָּה הַקְהֵה אֶת-שִׁנָּיו וֶאֱמוֹר לוֹ. בַּעֲבוּר זֶה עָשָׂה יְיָ לִי בְּצֵאתִי מִמִּצְרָיִם: לִי וְלֹא לוֹ. אִלּוּ הָיָה שָׁם לֹא הָיָה נִגְאָל:

תָּם מַה הוּא אוֹמֵר. מַה-זֹּאת. וְאָמַרְתָּ אֵלָיו. בְּחֹזֶק יָד הוֹצִיאָנוּ יְיָ מִמִּצְרַיִם מִבֵּית עֲבָדִים:

וְשֶׁאֵינוֹ יוֹדֵעַ לִשְׁאוֹל אַתְּ פְּתַח לוֹ. שֶׁנֶּאֱמַר: וְהִגַּדְתָּ לְבִנְךָ בַּיּוֹם הַהוּא לֵאמֹר. בַּעֲ־בוּר זֶה עָשָׂה יְיָ לִי בְּצֵאתִי מִמִּצְרָיִם:

יָכוֹל מֵרֹאשׁ חֹדֶשׁ. תַּלְמוּד לוֹמַר בַּיּוֹם הַהוּא. אִי בַּיּוֹם הַהוּא יָכוֹל מִבְּעוֹד יוֹם. תַּלְמוּד לוֹמַר. בַּעֲבוּר-זֶה. בַּעֲבוּר-זֶה לֹא אָמַרְתִּי אֶלָּא בְּשָׁעָה שֶׁיֵּשׁ מַצָּה וּמָרוֹר מֻנָּחִים לְפָנֶיךָ:

מִתְּחִלָּה עוֹבְדֵי כוֹכָבִים הָיוּ אֲבוֹתֵינוּ. וְעַכְשָׁו קֵרְבָנוּ הַמָּקוֹם לַעֲבוֹדָתוֹ. שֶׁנֶּאֱמַר: וַיֹּאמֶר יְהוֹשֻׁעַ אֶל-כָּל-הָעָם. כֹּה אָמַר יְיָ אֱלֹהֵי יִשְׂרָאֵל בְּעֵבֶר הַנָּהָר יָשְׁבוּ אֲבוֹתֵיכֶם מֵעוֹלָם תֶּרַח אֲבִי אַבְרָהָם וַאֲבִי נָחוֹר. וַיַּעַבְדוּ אֱלֹהִים אֲחֵרִים: וָאֶקַּח אֶת-אֲבִיכֶם אֶת-אַבְרָהָם מֵעֵבֶר הַנָּהָר. וָאוֹלֵךְ אוֹתוֹ בְּכָל-אֶרֶץ כְּנָעַן. וָאַרְבֶּה אֶת-זַרְעוֹ וָאֶתֶּן לוֹ אֶת-יִצְחָק: וָאֶתֵּן לְיִצְחָק אֶת-יַעֲקֹב וְאֶת-עֵשָׂו. וָאֶתֵּן לְעֵשָׂו אֶת-הַר שֵׂעִיר לָרֶשֶׁת אוֹתוֹ וְיַעֲקֹב וּבָנָיו יָרְדוּ מִצְרָיִם:

The Four Children

Blessed be the Omnipresent, blessed be He, who gave the Torah to his people Israel.

The Passover Story is interpreted in different ways by each generation. Therein its durability. That the Passover can be understood in different ways by different people can be seen in the example of the four children: one is intelligent, the second is wicked, the third is simple, and the fourth doesn't yet know how to ask.

WHAT DOES THE INTELLIGENT CHILD SAY?

"What are the meanings of the testimonies, statutes, and ordinances that God has commanded?"

And this child should be taught: "One shouldn't conclude the Passover meal with the statement, 'On to the entertainment!' Instead, one should stress the lasting meaning of storytelling."

WHAT DOES THE WAYWARD CHILD SAY?

"What is this service to you?"
Since this child removes himself or herself from the group, and thus seems to reject tradition, the answer ought to be: "It is because of that which God did for all of us when we came forth from Egypt. Had we all been there, the people of Israel would have been redeemed. Since we were not, knowledge has to pass from one generation to the next.

WHAT DOES THE SIMPLE CHILD SAY?

"What is this?" And you shall say: "By strength, God brought us out from Egypt, from the house of bondage."

AND WITH HIM WHO DOES NOT KNOW HOW TO ASK,

You must be vulnerable. "And you shalt tell your son and daughter, you might not know how to ask and sometimes I might not know how to answer. Not knowing is as important as knowing if it is understood that it leads to further understanding."

In the beginning our fathers and mothers were ignorant, but now they inquire about the meaning of the Passover story. "And Joshua said to all the people: 'Thus says the God of Israel: Your fathers dwelt of old time beyond the River, even Terah, the father of Abraham, and the father of Nahor; and they served other gods. And I took your father Abraham from beyond the River, and led him throughout all the land of Canaan, and multiplied his seed, and gave him Isaac. And I gave unto Isaac Jacob and Esau; and I have given Mount Seir to Esau, to possess it; and Jacob and his children went down into Egypt'."

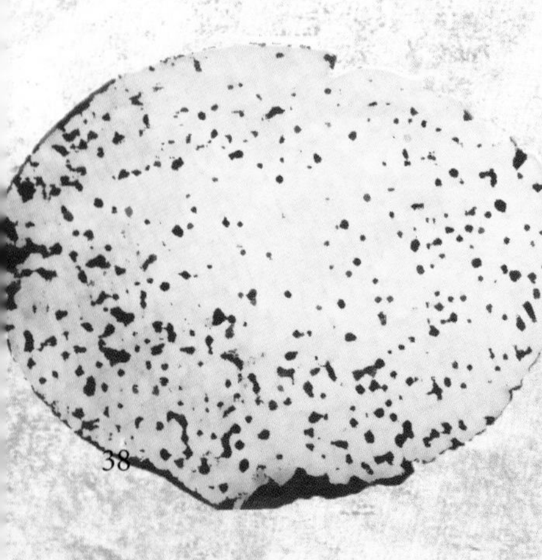

The Ten Plagues

↫ The head of the table and all of those present list the ten plagues while dipping a finger in the cup of wine and placing a drop on their plate for each. ↬

These are the ten plagues God sent against Pharaoh and the people of Egypt.

The plagues are a reminder of our enslavement in Egypt and the commitment by God to help us achieve freedom. In Passover, every generation of Jews relives the bondage we suffered and embraced the desire for liberation, for the Jewish people as well as for the whole of humanity.

5

דֶּבֶר

Dever

Diseased livestock

6

שְׁחִין

Sh'chin

Boils

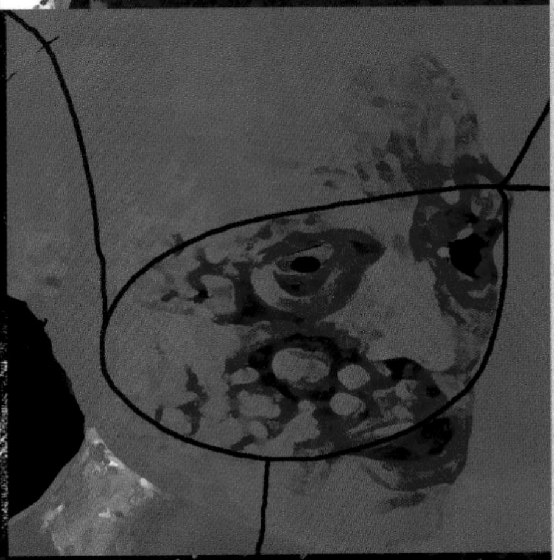

7

בָּרָד

Barad

Hail

8

אַרְבֶּה

Arbeh

Locusts

9

חוֹשֶׁךְ

Choshech

Darkness

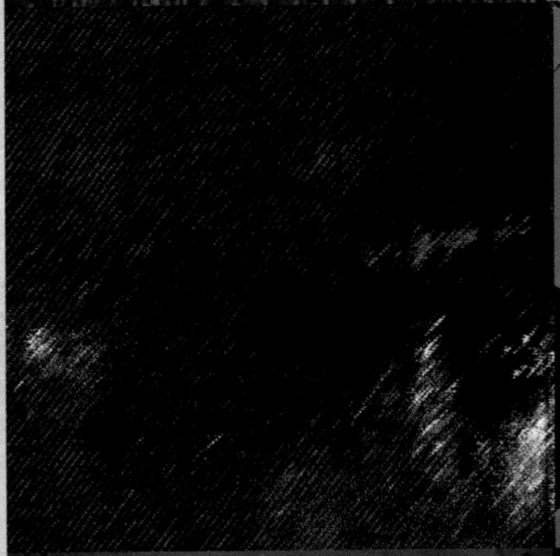

10

מַכַּת בְּכוֹרוֹת

Makat Bechorot

Death of firstborn

THE HEAD OF THE TABLE READS THE TWO POEMS ON THE NEXT PAGE ABOUT BONDAGE, BOTH PHYSICAL AND EMOTIONAL.

João Pinto Delgado

(1580-1653)

Born in Portugal. *Converso* poet who migrated to Amsterdam and returned to Judaism.

La Salida de Egipto

(Spanish/English)

En este fiero Egipto
de mi pecado, donde el alma mía
padece la tirana servidumbre,
del tesoro infinito
de tu divina lumbre,
a mi noche, Señor, un rayo envía,
sea tu santa inspiración mi guía;
que entre la luz del amoroso fuego
me llame en el desierto, no cursado
de mundana memoria:
allí desnudo, por tu causa, el ciego
velo de error, el hábito pasado,
dichoso suba a contemplar tu gloria,
donde mi ser por milagroso efeto
en sí transforme el soberano objeto.

. . . . .

Departure from Egypt

In this fierce Egypt
of my sin, where my soul
suffers the tyrannical servitude,
of the infinite treasure
of your divine flame,
may you send, Master, a ray,
may your holy inspiration be my guide;
so that the light of your loving fire
may call upon me in the desert, not coursed
in mundane memory:
therein naked, for your cause, in the blind
veil of error, the past habit,
may I ascend in joy to contemplate your glory,
where my being by miraculous effect
may become in itself a sovereign object.

— Translation Ilan Stavans

Love and Freedom

I Love the Love in You

Ilan Stavans

I love the love in you.

I love your smile,
your eyes,
your lips,
your hair,
the freedom that you share,
I love the way you are.

I love your warmth.
your peace
your strength,
your fairness.
I love your rhythm,
the way you sleep with me,
the softness of your skin.

I love the way you love.
I love the love in you.

I love your trust in love.

Pesach, Matzah, Maror

רַבָּן גַּמְלִיאֵל הָיָה אוֹמֵר: כָּל שֶׁלֹּא אָמַר שְׁלשָׁה דְּבָרִים אֵלּוּ בַּפֶּסַח, לֹא יָצָא יְדֵי חוֹבָתוֹ, וְאֵלּוּ הֵן.

פֶּסַח, מַצָּה, וּמָרוֹר

Rabban Gamaliel used to say: "Whoever does not make mention of the following three things on Passover has not fulfilled his obligation: the Passover Sacrifice, unleavened bread, and bitter herbs."

פֶּסַח שֶׁהָיוּ אֲבוֹתֵינוּ אוֹכְלִים בִּזְמַן שֶׁבֵּית הַמִּקְדָּשׁ הָיָה קַיָּם עַל-שׁוּם מָה? עַל-שׁוּם שֶׁפָּסַח הַקָּדוֹשׁ בָּרוּךְ הוּא עַל-בָּתֵּי אבוֹתֵינוּ בְּמִצְרַיִם. שֶׁנֶּאֱמַר: וַאֲמַרְתֶּם זֶבַח-פֶּסַח הוּא לַיְיָ אֲשֶׁר פָּסַח עַל-בָּתֵּי בְנֵי-יִשְׂרָאֵל בְּמִצְרַיִם בְּנָגְפּוֹ אֶת-מִצְרַיִם וְאֶת-בָּתֵּינוּ הִצִּיל. וַיִּקֹּד הָעָם וַיִּשְׁתַּחֲווּ:

What was the reason for eating the Passover Sacrifice, which our fathers and mothers used to eat at the time when the Holy Temple still stood? Because the Holy One, blessed be He, passed over the houses of our fathers and mothers in Egypt.

As it is said: "It is the sacrifice of God's Passover, for God passed over the houses of the children of Israel in Egypt, smote the Egyptians, and delivered us from bondage. And the people bowed the head and worshiped."

THE HEAD OF THE TABLE LIFTS THE MATZAH *AND SAYS:.*

מַצָּה זוֹ שֶׁאָנוּ אוֹכְלִים
עַל-שׁוּם מָה? עַל-שׁוּם
שֶׁלֹּא הִסְפִּיק בְּצֵקָם שֶׁל-
אֲבוֹתֵינוּ לְהַחֲמִיץ עַד-
שֶׁנִּגְלָה עֲלֵיהֶם מֶלֶךְ מַלְכֵי
הַמְּלָכִים הַקָּדוֹשׁ בָּרוּךְ
הוּא וּגְאָלָם, שֶׁנֶּאֱמַר:
וַיֹּאפוּ אֶת-הַבָּצֵק אֲשֶׁר
הוֹצִיאוּ מִמִּצְרַיִם עֻגֹת
מַצּוֹת כִּי לֹא חָמֵץ. כִּי-
גֹרְשׁוּ מִמִּצְרַיִם וְלֹא יָכְלוּ
לְהִתְמַהְמֵהַּ וְגַם-צֵדָה לֹא-
עָשׂוּ לָהֶם:

This matzah which we eat, what is the reason for it? Because the dough of our ancestors had not yet leavened when the Master over all kings, the Holy One, blessed be He, revealed himself to them and redeemed them.

As it is said: "And they baked unleavened cakes of the dough which they brought forth out of Egypt, for it was not leavened; because they were thrust out of Egypt, and could not tarry, neither had they prepared for themselves any victual."

THE HEAD OF THE TABLE LIFTS THE BITTER HERBS.

These bitter herbs we eat,
what is the reason for them?
Because the Egyptians made the lives
of our ancestors bitter in Egypt.
As it is said: "And they made their lives bitter
with hard service, in mortar and in brick,
and in all manner of service in the field;
in all their service, wherein they made
them serve with rigor."

מָרוֹר זֶה שֶׁאָנוּ אוֹכְלִים עַל-
שׁוּם מָה? עַל-שׁוּם שֶׁמֵּרְרוּ
הַמִּצְרִים אֶת-חַיֵּי אֲבוֹתֵינוּ
בְּמִצְרָיִם שֶׁנֶּאֱמַר: וַיְמָרְרוּ אֶת-
חַיֵּיהֶם בַּעֲבוֹדָה קָשָׁה, בְּחֹמֶר
וּבִלְבֵנִים, וּבְכָל-עֲבֹדָה בַּשָּׂדֶה.
אֵת כָּל-עֲבֹדָתָם אֲשֶׁר-עָבְדוּ
בָהֶם בְּפָרֶךְ:

In Every Generation

The head of the table explains that exodus and redemption not only took place in bygone days but continue to be part of contemporary life.

בְּכָל-דּוֹר וָדוֹר חַיָּב אָדָם
לִרְאוֹת אֶת-עַצְמוֹ כְּאִלּוּ הוּא
יָצָא מִמִּצְרָיִם, שֶׁנֶּאֱמַר: וְהִגַּ-
דְתָּ לְבִנְךָ בַּיּוֹם הַהוּא לֵאמֹר.
בַּעֲבוּר זֶה עָשָׂה יְיָ לִי בְּצֵאתִי
מִמִּצְרָיִם: לֹא אֶת-אֲבוֹתֵינוּ
בִּלְבַד גָּאַל הַקָּדוֹשׁ בָּרוּךְ הוּא.
אֶלָּא אַף אוֹתָנוּ גָּאַל עִמָּהֶם.
שֶׁנֶּאֱמַר: וְאוֹתָנוּ הוֹצִיא מִשָּׁם,
לְמַעַן הָבִיא אוֹתָנוּ לָתֶת לָנוּ
אֶת-הָאָרֶץ אֲשֶׁר נִשְׁבַּע לַאֲבֹ-
תֵינוּ

In every generation, let each person look as if he came forth out of Egypt.
As it is said: "And you shall tell your son and daughter in that day, saying: 'It is because of that which God did for me when I came forth out of Egypt.'"
It was not only our fathers and mothers that God redeemed, but us as well did God redeem along with them.
As it is said: "And God brought us out from thence, that God might bring us in, to give us the land swore unto our ancestors."
… eat of the sacrifices and the paschal offerings, whose blood will come unto the walls of thy altar for acceptance. Then shall we give thanks to You with a new song, for our redemption and the liberation of our soul.

Say the following blessing.

בָּרוּךְ אַתָּה יְיָ אֱלֹהֵינוּ מֶלֶךְ הָעוֹלָם בּוֹרֵא פְּרִי הַגָּפֶן

Blessed are You, our God, master of the universe, creator of the fruit of the vine.

Drink the second cup of wine while in a reclining position.

WASH HANDS AND SAY THE FOLLOWING BLESSING.

רָחְצָה

בָּרוּךְ אַתָּה יְיָ אֱלֹהֵינוּ מֶלֶךְ הָעוֹלָם אֲשֶׁר קִדְּשָׁנוּ בְּמִצְוֹתָיו וְצִוָּנוּ עַל נְטִי־לַת יָדָיִם

Wash Hands

BLESSED are You, our God, master of the universe, who sanctified us with the commandments and commanded us in the washing of hands.

THE HEAD OF THE TABLE BREAKS PIECES FROM THE UPPER AND MIDDLE MATZAHS AND DISTRIBUTES THEM.

SAY THE FOLLOWING BLESSINGS.

בָּרוּךְ אַתָּה יְיָ אֱלֹהֵינוּ מֶלֶךְ הָעוֹלָם הַמּוֹצִיא לֶחֶם מִן הָאָרֶץ

בָּרוּךְ אַתָּה יְיָ אֱלֹהֵינוּ מֶלֶךְ הָעוֹלָם אֲשֶׁר קִדְּשָׁנוּ בְּמִצְוֹתָיו וְצִוָּנוּ עַל אֲכִי־לַת מַצָּה

BLESSED are You, our God, master of the universe, who brings forth bread from the earth.
BLESSED are You, our God, master of the universe, who sanctified us with the commandments and commanded us to eat unleavened bread.

THE MATZAH IS EATEN IN A RECLINING POSITION.

Hillel Sandwich

The head of the table dips bitter herbs in the *haroset* and offers a piece to each person. This combination is the Hillel Sandwich, named after the Babylonian sage and scholar who died in 10 C.E.

Say the following blessing before eating the bitter herbs.

בָּרוּךְ אַתָּה יְיָ אֱלֹהֵינוּ מֶלֶךְ הָעוֹלָם אֲשֶׁר קִדְּשָׁנוּ בְּמִצְוֹתָיו וְצִוָּנוּ עַל אֲכִילַת מָרוֹר:

BLESSED are You, our God, master of the universe,
who sanctified us with the commandments and commanded us to eat bitter herbs

The head of the table breaks the bottom matzah, then puts bitter herbs sandwich-fashion between two pieces of matzah. The following is recited before eating.

זֵכֶר לְמִקְדָּשׁ כְּהִלֵּל: כֵּן עָשָׂה הִלֵּל בִּזְמַן שֶׁבֵּית הַמִּקְדָּשׁ הָיָה קַיָּם. הָיָה כּוֹרֵךְ [פֶּסַח] מַצָּה וּמָרוֹר וְאוֹכֵל בְּיַחַד. לְקַיֵּם מַה שֶּׁנֶּאֱמַר: עַל-מַצּוֹת וּמְרֹרִים יֹאכְלֻהוּ:

In memory of the Temple, according to the custom of Hillel. Thus did Hillel when the Holy Temple still stood: he used to combine unleavened bread and bitter herbs and eat them together, to fulfill that which is said: "They shall eat it with unleavened bread and bitter herbs."

The Seder plate is removed.

The story is paused and food is served.

Enjoy the Meal

with family and friends.

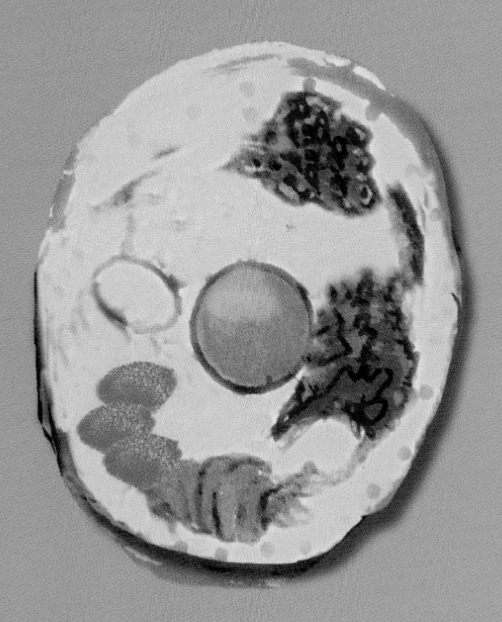

שֻׁלְחָן עוֹרֵךְ

Shulchan Orech

At the beginning of the meal,
boiled eggs in salt water are eaten.

מצה
פסח

After the Meal

We Celebrate Our Freedoms

The Seder plate is again placed on the table.

The head of the table asks someone to recite the poems on the following pages.

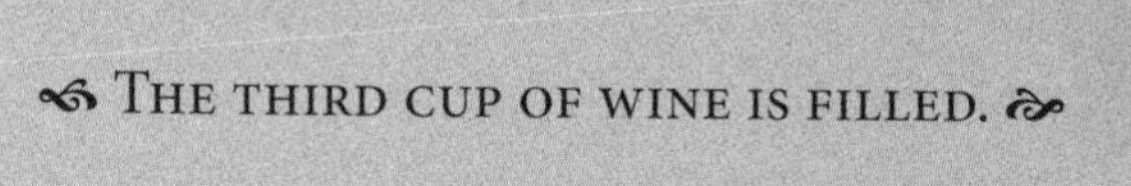

The third cup of wine is filled.

Our Dreams

Ilan Stavans

Every night, as we close our eyes,
we are free
and the world starts anew.

In the realm of dreams,
there is no past,
everything happens at once,
night is day,
people are ghosts,
we are happy
and the world is ours.

Every night, as we close our eyes,
we are out of Egypt,
lead by Moses
onto the Promised Land

In the realm of dreams,
the lamb sits next to the lion,
the land is plentiful,
the air is clean,
and the water fresh.

And then our eyes reopen.

Auschwitz

Ilan Stavans

The line is long:
as long as it lasts, death won't come...

The over door is wide open,
the fire inside is eternal.
An SS meticulously checks all documents.
A drop of sweat in his forehead
stubbornly makes its way down.
The shadow of a fly pullulates
on the nervous ground.

Our enemies will ever cease;
their hatred is constant.
It validates us.
Every man is the first man
and the last.
Our ancestors are ashes now
as are our successors.
Should we hate, too? Is hatred
the fuel on which
the world moves?

Why do we need to be fragile?
Why do we feel alone?
In suffering the source of meaning?

The line is long:
as long as it lasts, death won't come…

LIFT THE THIRD CUP OF WINE AND SAY THE FOLLOWING BLESSING.

בָּרוּךְ אַתָּה יְיָ אֱלֹהֵינוּ מֶלֶךְ הָעוֹלָם בּוֹרֵא פְּרִי הַגָּפֶן

BLESSED are You, our God, Master of the Universe, creator of the fruit of the vine.

DRINK THE CUP OF WINE WHILE IN A RECLINING POSITION.

THE HEAD OF THE TABLE INVITES DIFFERENT PARTICIPANTS TO TALK ABOUT THE DISTRESS OF JEWS IN EUROPE AND THE AMERICAS AND HOW JEWS HAVE RESPONDED WITH LIFE GIVING ENERGY — FROM THE EXPULSIONS OF JEWS FROM COUNTRIES, NOTABLY SPAIN, TO RUSSIAN POGROMS, THE HEINOUS EVENTS OF THE HOLOCAUST, AND THE TERRORIST ATTACKS OF RECENT DECADES, SUCH AS THE 1994 BOMBING OF THE JEWISH COMMUNITY CENTER, AMIA (ASOCIACIÓN MUTUAL ISRAELITA ARGENTINA), IN BUENOS AIRES.

Mordechai Gebirtig

(1877-1942)
Yiddish folksong of persecution

S'brent/ס׳ברענט

ס׳ברענט! ברידערלעך, ס׳ברענט!
אוי, אונדזער אָרעם שטעטל נעבעך
ברענט!
בייזע ווינטן מיט ירגזון
רײַסן, ברעכן און צעבלאָזן
שטארקער נאָך די ווילדע פֿלאַמען
אַלץ אַרום שוין ברענט!

און איר שטייט און קוקט אַזוי זיך
מיט פֿאַרלייגטע הענט.
און איר שטייט און קוקט אַזוי זיך -
אונדזער שטעטל ברענט...

ס׳ברענט! ברידערלעך, ס׳ברענט!
אוי, אונדזער אָרעם שטעטל נעבעך
ברענט!
ס׳האָבן שוין די פֿײַער-צונגען
דאָס גאַנצע שטעטל איינגעשלונגען -
און די בייזע ווינטן הודזשען
אונדזער שטעטל ברענט!

ס׳ברענט! ברידערלעך, ס׳ברענט!
אוי, עס קען חלילה קומען דער מאָמענט:
אונדזער שטאָט מיט אונדז צוזאַמען
זאָל אויף אַש אַוועק אין פֿלאַמען
בלײַבן זאָל - ווי נאָך אַ שלאַכט
נאָר פּוסטע, שוואַרצע ווענט!

ס׳ברענט! ברידערלעך, ס׳ברענט!
די הילף איז נאָר אין אייך אַליין
געווענדט!
אייב דאס שטעטל א׳ז אייך טײַער
נעמט ד׳ ק׳ל׳ם, לעשט דאָס פֿײַער
לעשט מ׳ט אייער אייגן בלוט
באַווײַזט אַז איר דאָס קענט.

שטייט ניט, ברידער, אָט אווי זיך
מיט פֿאַרלייגטע הענט.
שטייט ניט, ברידער, לעשט דאָס פֿײַער
אונדזער שטעטל ברענט!

It's Burning

It's burning, brothers! It's burning!
Oh, our poor village, brothers, burns!
Evil winds, full of anger,
Rage and ravage, smash and shatter;
Stronger now that wild flames grow --
All around now burns!
And you stand there looking on
With futile, folded arms
And you stand there looking on --
While our village burns!
It's burning, brothers! It's burning!
Oh, our poor village, brothers, burns!
Soon the rabid tongues of fire
Will consume each house entire,
As the wild wind blows and howls --
The whole town's up in flames!
And you stand there looking on
With futile, folded arms,
And you stand there looking on --
While our village burns!

It's burning, brothers! Our town is burning!
Oh, God forbid the moment should arrive,
That our town, with us, together,
Should go up in ash and fire,
Leaving when the slaughter's ended
Charred and empty walls!
And you stand there looking on
With futile, folded arms,
And you stand there looking on --
While our village burns!
It's burning, brothers! Our town is burning!
And our salvation hands on you alone.
If our town is dear to you,
Grab the buckets, douse the fire!
Show that you know how!
Don't stand there, brothers, looking on
With futile, folded arms,
Don't stand there, brothers, douse the fire! --
Our poor village burns!

— Translation Ilan Stavans

The door is opened and the youngest child calls to the Prophet Elijah to come in.

Continue with the following.

שְׁפֹךְ חֲמָתְךָ אֶל הַגּוֹיִם אֲשֶׁר לֹא יְדָעוּךָ. וְעַל מַמְלָכוֹת אֲשֶׁר
בְּשִׁמְךָ לֹא קָרָאוּ: כִּי אָכַל אֶת יַעֲקֹב וְאֶת נָוֵהוּ הֵשַׁמּוּ: שְׁפָךְ
עֲלֵיהֶם זַעְמֶךָ וַחֲרוֹן אַפְּךָ יַשִּׂיגֵם: תִּרְדֹּף בְּאַף וְתַשְׁמִידֵם, מִתַּחַת
שְׁמֵי יְיָ:

Pour out Your wrath upon the nations that know You not, and upon the kingdoms that call not upon Your name. For they have devoured Jacob, and laid waste his habitation. Pour out Your indignation upon them, and let the fierceness of Your anger overtake them. Pursue them in anger, and destroy them, from under God's heavens.

Fill the fourth cup of wine.

The head of the table explains that the plight of any slave anywhere is to be remembered like the bondage Jews underwent in Egypt.

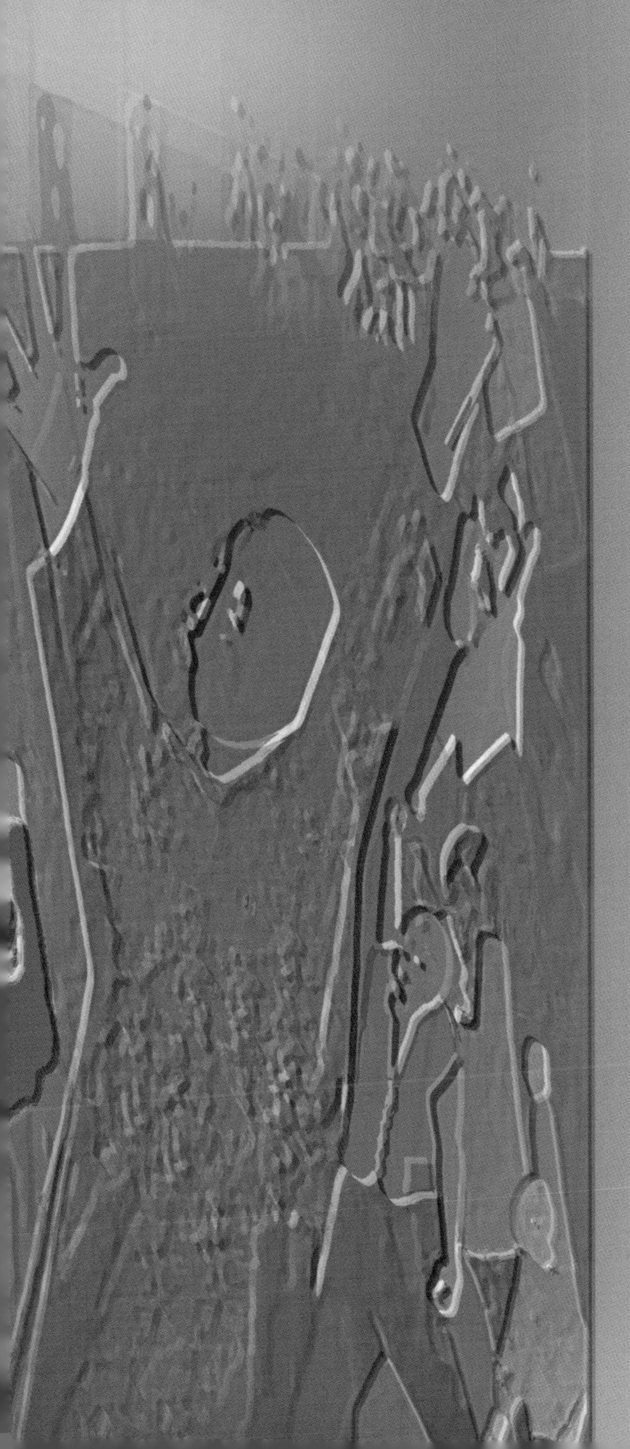

We Shall Overcome

This became a protest song and a key anthem of the African American Civil Rights Movement (1955–1968).

We shall overcome, we shall overcome,
We shall overcome someday;
Oh, deep in my heart, I do believe,
We shall overcome someday.

The Lord will see us through, The Lord will see us through,
The Lord will see us through someday;
Oh, deep in my heart, I do believe,
We shall overcome someday.
We're on to victory, We're on to victory,
We're on to victory someday;
Oh, deep in my heart, I do believe,
We're on to victory someday.

We'll walk hand in hand, we'll walk hand in hand,
We'll walk hand in hand someday;
Oh, deep in my heart, I do believe,
We'll walk hand in hand someday.

We are not afraid, we are not afraid,
We are not afraid today;
Oh, deep in my heart, I do believe,
We are not afraid today.

The truth shall make us free, the truth shall make us free,
The truth shall make us free someday;
Oh, deep in my heart, I do believe,
The truth shall make us free someday.

We shall live in peace, we shall live in peace,
We shall live in peace someday;
Oh, deep in my heart, I do believe,
We shall live in peace someday.

The head of the table leads in the following:

אוֹדְךָ כִּי עֲנִיתָנִי וַתְּהִי לִי לִישׁוּעָה.
אֶבֶן מָאֲסוּ הַבּוֹנִים. הָיְתָה לְרֹאשׁ פִּנָּה.
אֶבֶן מָאֲסוּ הַבּוֹנִים הָיְתָה לְרֹאשׁ פִּנָּה.
מֵאֵת יְיָ הָיְתָה זֹּאת הִיא נִפְלָאת בְּעֵינֵינוּ.

I will give thanks unto You, for you have answered me and become my salvation.
The stone which the builders rejected is become the chief corner-stone.
This is God's doing; it is marvelous in our eyes.
This is the day that God has made. We will rejoice and be glad in it.

אָנָּא יְיָ הוֹשִׁיעָה נָּא.
אָנָּא יְיָ הוֹשִׁיעָה נָּא.
אָנָּא יְיָ הַצְלִיחָה נָּא.
אָנָּא יְיָ הַצְלִיחָה נָּא.

We beseech You, O God, save us now!
We beseech You, O God, save us now!
We beseech You, O God, make us now to prosper!
We beseech You, O God, make us now to prosper!

Lift the fourth cup of wine and say the following blessing.

בָּרוּךְ אַתָּה יְיָ אֱלֹהֵינוּ מֶלֶךְ הָעוֹלָם בּוֹרֵא פְּרִי הַגָּפֶן

Blessed are You, our God, Master of the Universe, creator of the fruit of the vine.

Drink the fourth cup of wine while in a reclining position.

Israel

Ilan Stavans

You were chosen
to be upright,
to be different,
to be better.

You were chosen
to upheld the law,
to love thy neighbor,
to be yourself

Your people aren't people
but models,
your leaders aren't leaders
but prophets.
You will always carry bondage in you.

You were chosen
to ask the questions
for which there are no answers.

דַּיֵּנוּ

(Aramaic/English)

אִלּוּ הוֹצִיאָנוּ מִמִּצְרַיִם, דַּיֵּנוּ
וְלֹא עָשָׂה בָהֶם שְׁפָטִים, דַּיֵּנוּ
אִלּוּ עָשָׂה בָהֶם שְׁפָטִים וְלֹא עָשָׂה בֵאלֹהֵיהֶם, דַּיֵּנוּ
אִלּוּ עָשָׂה בֵאלֹהֵיהֶם וְלֹא הָרַג אֶת בְּכוֹרֵיהֶם, דַּיֵּנוּ
אִלּוּ הָרַג אֶת בְּכוֹרֵיהֶם וְלֹא נָתַן לָנוּ אֶת מָמוֹנָם, דַּיֵּנוּ
אִלּוּ נָתַן לָנוּ אֶת מָמוֹנָם וְלֹא קָרַע לָנוּ אֶת הַיָּם, דַּיֵּנוּ
אִלּוּ קָרַע לָנוּ אֶת הַיָּם וְלֹא הֶעֱבִירָנוּ בְתוֹכוֹ בֶּחָרָבָה, דַּיֵּנוּ
אִלּוּ הֶעֱבִירָנוּ בְתוֹכוֹ בֶּחָרָבָה וְלֹא שִׁקַּע צָרֵינוּ בְּתוֹכוֹ, דַּיֵּנוּ
אִלּוּ שִׁקַּע צָרֵינוּ בְּתוֹכוֹ וְלֹא סִפֵּק צָרְכֵּנוּ בַּמִּדְבָּר אַרְבָּעִים שָׁנָה, דַּיֵּנוּ
אִלּוּ סִפֵּק צָרְכֵּנוּ בַּמִּדְבָּר אַרְבָּעִים שָׁנָה וְלֹא הֶאֱכִילָנוּ אֶת הַמָּן, דַּיֵּנוּ
אִלּוּ הֶאֱכִילָנוּ אֶת הַמָּן וְלֹא נָתַן לָנוּ אֶת הַשַּׁבָּת, דַּיֵּנוּ
אִלּוּ נָתַן לָנוּ אֶת הַשַּׁבָּת וְלֹא קֵרְבָנוּ לִפְנֵי הַר סִינַי, דַּיֵּנוּ
אִלּוּ קֵרְבָנוּ לִפְנֵי הַר סִינַי וְלֹא נָתַן לָנוּ אֶת הַתּוֹרָה, דַּיֵּנוּ
אִלּוּ נָתַן לָנוּ אֶת הַתּוֹרָה וְלֹא הִכְנִיסָנוּ לְאֶרֶץ יִשְׂרָאֵל, דַּיֵּנוּ
אִלּוּ הִכְנִיסָנוּ לְאֶרֶץ יִשְׂרָאֵל וְלֹא בָנָה לָנוּ אֶת בֵּית הַמִּקְדָּשׁ. דַּיֵּנוּ

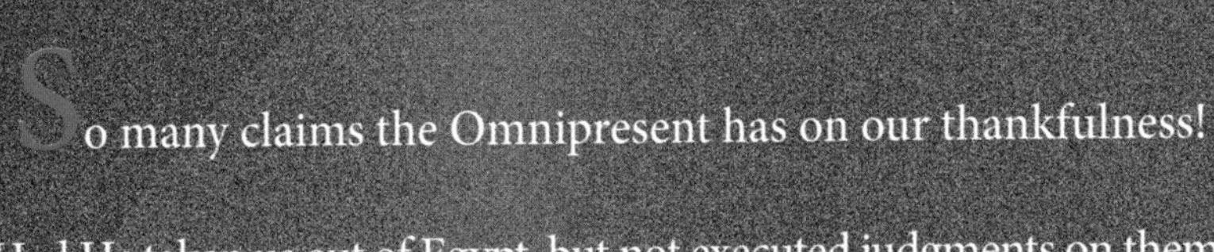

So many claims the Omnipresent has on our thankfulness!

Had He taken us out of Egypt, but not executed judgments on them,
Dayeinu.
(We should have been content!)
Had He executed judgments on them, but not upon their gods,
Dayeinu.
Had He executed judgments on their gods, but not slain their first born,
Dayeinu.
Had He slain their first-born, but not given us their substance,
Dayeinu.
Had He given us their substance, but not torn the Sea apart for us,
Dayeinu.
Had He torn the Sea apart for us, but not brought us through it dry,
Dayeinu.
Had He brought us through it dry, but not sunk our oppressors in the midst of it,
Dayeinu.
Had He sunk our oppressors in the midst of it,
but not satisfied our needs in the desert for forty years,
Dayeinu.
Had He satisfied our needs in the desert for forty years, but not fed us manna,
Dayeinu.
Had He fed us manna, but not given us the Sabbath,
Dayeinu.
Had He given us the Sabbath, but not brought us to Mount Sinai,
Dayeinu.
Had He brought us to Mount Sinai, but not given us the Torah,
Dayeinu.
Had He given us the Torah, but not brought us into the Land of Israel,
Dayeinu.
Had He brought us into the Land of Israel, but not built us the House of His choosing,
Dayeinu.

De colores

(Spanish/English)

Traditional religious Spanish ballad brought to the Americas during the 17th century. In the 1960s, the United Farm Workers Union adopted the song as a hymn in its struggle for justice and equality.

De colores, de colores se visten los campos en la primavera.
De colores, de colores son los pajaritos que vienen de fuera.
De colores, de colores es el arco iris que vemos lucir.
Y por eso los grandes amores de muchos colores me gustan a mí.
Y por eso los grandes amores de muchos colores me gustan a mí.
Canta el gallo, canta el gallo con el kikirikí.
La gallina, la gallina con el cara cara cara cara.
Los pollitos, los pollitos con el pío pío pío pí.
Y por eso los grandes amores de muchos colores me gustan a mí.
Y por eso los grandes amores de muchos colores me gustan a mí.
De colores, de colores brillantes y finos se viste la aurora.
De colores, de colores son los mil reflejos que el sol atesora.
De colores, de colores se viste el diamante que vemos lucir.
Y por eso los grandes amores de muchos colores me gustan a mí.
Y por eso los grandes amores de muchos colores me gustan a mí.
Jubilosos, jubilosos vivamos en gracia puesto que se puede.
Saciaremos, saciaremos la sed ardorosa del ley que no muere.
Jubilosos, jubilosos llevemos a Dios un alma y mil más.
Difundiendo la luz que ilumina la gracia divina del gran ideal.
Difundiendo la luz que ilumina la gracia divina del gran ideal.

In Such Colors

In such colors, in such colors the countryside dresses itself in spring's graces.
In such colors, in such colors the birds come to us from such faraway places.
In such colors, in such colors the rainbow shines brightly in our eyes.
It's enchanting, great love and its colors, great love and its colors, this love I would see.
It's enchanting, great love and its colors, great love and its colors, this love I would see.

The cock is crowing, the cock crows his cock-doodle-doo-doo-doo-doo.
The hen is clucking, the hen clucks her cluck, cluck, cluck, cluck.

The chicks are peeping, the chicks peep their peep, peep, peep, peep,.
It's enchanting, great love and its colors, great love and its colors, this love I would see.
It's enchanting, great love and its colors, great love and its colors, this love I would see.

In such colors, in such colors the sky dresses up in its finest at sunrise.
In such colors, in such colors the sun sends back all the treasures we longed for.
In such colors, in such colors a diamond dresses itself up in our eyes.
It's enchanting, great love and its colors, great love and its colors, this love I would see.
It's enchanting, great love and its colors, great love and its colors, this love I would see.

Jubilation, jubilation we aim for no matter the lives that confront us.
We will ease it, we will ease the great thirsting of the law that's immortal.
Jubilation, jubilation will give God one soul and many thousands more.
As we spread all the light that illumines God's grace and His great ideals evermore.
As we spread all the light that illumines God's grace and His great ideals evermore.

— Translation Ilan Stavans

Traditional Afro-American Spiritual

This became a leading chant during marches and protests in the Civil Rights Movement in the United States in the 1960s.

Let my people go

(English)

When Israel was in Egypt's land, Let my people go.
Oppressed so hard they could not stand, Let my people go

Go down, Moses, Way down in Egypt's land,
Tell old Pharaoh, "Let my people go."

"Thus says the Lord," bold Moses said, "Let my people go.
If not I'll smite your first born dead, Let my people go."

Go down, Moses, Way down in Egypt's land
Tell old Pharaoh, Let my people go.

The Lord told Moses what to do, Let my people go
To lead the children of Israel through, Let my people go.

Go down, Moses, Way down in Egypt's land
Tell old Pharaoh, "Let my people go."

When they had reached the other shore, Let my people go
They sang a song of triumph o'er, Let my people go.

Go down, Moses, Way down in Egypt's land,
Tell old Pharaoh, "Let my people go."

THE HEAD OF THE TABLE INVITES THE CHILDREN TO LOOK FOR THE *AFIKOMAN* WITH A REWARD FOR THE ONE WHO FINDS IT.

Traditional Sephardic text

For centuries, this song has been an integral part of Sephardic Seders from Jerusalem to Mexico City.

Moses Left Egypt

Moses left Misrayim fleeing from King Paro
He went straight to Midian and found Yitro.
He gave him Sipora, his daughter because he feared God
Moses herded the cattle that his father-in-law gave him
Moses, herding the cattle, arrived to Mount Horeb
He saw a bush burning but was not consumed.
Moses covered his eyes fearing to see God
He heard a voice that said Moses, Moses, my servant
Take off your shoes you are standing in a holy place
You will go straight to Misrayim and tell King Paro
To give you the keys of my people, the Hebrews
And if he does not give them I will punish him
With ten plagues that I will send so he knows who I am.
Give thanks to the Lord for His goodness is ever present
Praise be His name because He has always been good to us
And in the heavens and on the earth, His mercy has
never been missing.

— Translation Vanessa Paloma Elbaz

Mose Salió de Misrayim

(Haketía/English)

Mose salió de Misrayim huyendo del Rey Paró
Se fue derecho a Midián y se encontró con Yitró
Le dió a Siporá su hija porque era teniente a Dio
Mose pasía el ganado que su suegro le entregó
Mose paciendo el ganado al monte de Horeb llegó
Viera ardir una zarza, la zarza no se quemó
Oyó una voz que dezía Mosé Mosé mi siervo
descalzate tus zapatos que en lugar santo estás tu.
Te irás derecho a Misrayim y dirás al Rey Paró
que te entregue las llaves, de mi pueblo el Hebreo
Y si no te las diera castigarle quiero yo
con diez plagas que le mande pa' que sepa quien soy yo
Hodu l'Ad-nai ki tov ki le'Olam jasdó
Alabado sea su nombre porque siempre bien nos dio
y en los cielos y en las tierras su merced nunca faltó.

Songs of Joy and Play

Who Knows One?

There are versions in several languages of this cumulative children's song, which probably appeared in Germany in the fifteenth century and might be rooted in the folksong *Guter freund ich frage dich*, meaning "Good friend, I ask you."

אֶחָד מִי יוֹדֵעַ

(Hebrew/English)

אֶחָד מִי יוֹדֵעַ?
אֶחָד אֲנִי יוֹדֵעַ
אֶחָד אֱלֹהֵינוּ שֶׁבַּשָּׁמַיִם וּבָאָרֶץ,

שְׁנַיִם מִי יוֹדֵעַ?
שְׁנַיִם אֲנִי יוֹדֵעַ: שְׁנֵי לֻחוֹת הַבְּרִית, אֶחָד אֱלֹהֵינוּ שֶׁבַּשָּׁמַיִם וּבָאָרֶץ.

שְׁלֹשָׁה מִי יוֹדֵעַ?
שְׁלֹשָׁה אֲנִי יוֹדֵעַ: שְׁלֹשָׁה אָבוֹת, שְׁנֵי לֻחוֹת הַבְּרִית, אֶחָד אֱלֹהֵינוּ שֶׁבַּשָּׁמַיִם וּבָאָרֶץ.

אַרְבַּע מִי יוֹדֵעַ?
אַרְבַּע אֲנִי יוֹדֵעַ: אַרְבַּע אִמָּהוֹת, שְׁלֹשָׁה אָבוֹת, שְׁנֵי לֻחוֹת הַבְּרִית, אֶחָד אֱלֹהֵינוּ שֶׁבַּשָּׁמַיִם וּבָאָרֶץ.

חֲמִשָּׁה מִי יוֹדֵעַ?
חֲמִשָּׁה אֲנִי יוֹדֵעַ: חֲמִשָּׁה חוּמְשֵׁי תוֹרָה, אַרְבַּע אִמָּהוֹת, שְׁלֹשָׁה אָבוֹת, שְׁנֵי לֻחוֹת הַבְּרִית, אֶחָד אֱלֹהֵינוּ שֶׁבַּשָּׁמַיִם וּבָאָרֶץ.

שִׁשָּׁה מִי יוֹדֵעַ?
שִׁשָּׁה אֲנִי יוֹדֵעַ: שִׁשָּׁה סִדְרֵי מִשְׁנָה, חֲמִשָּׁה חוּמְשֵׁי תוֹרָה, אַרְבַּע אִמָּהוֹת, שְׁלֹשָׁה אָבוֹת, שְׁנֵי לֻחוֹת הַבְּרִית, אֶחָד אֱלֹהֵינוּ שֶׁבַּשָּׁמַיִם וּבָאָרֶץ.

שִׁבְעָה מִי יוֹדֵעַ?
שִׁבְעָה אֲנִי יוֹדֵעַ: שִׁבְעָה יְמֵי שַׁבַּתָּא' שִׁשָּׁה סִדְרֵי מִשְׁנָה' חֲמִשָּׁה חוּמְשֵׁי תוֹרָה' אַרְבַּע אִמָּהוֹת' שְׁלֹשָׁה אָבוֹת' שְׁנֵי לֻחוֹת הַבְּרִית' אֶחָד אֱלֹהֵימוּ שֶׁבַּשָּׁמַיִם וּבָאָרֶץ.

שְׁמוֹנָה מִי יוֹדֵעַ?
שְׁמוֹנָה אֲנִי יוֹדֵעַ: שְׁמוֹנָה יְמֵי מִילָה, שִׁבְעָה יְמֵי שַׁבַּתָּא, שִׁשָּׁה סִדְרֵי מִשְׁנָה, חֲמִשָּׁה חוּמְשֵׁי תוֹרָה, אַרְבַּע אִמָּהוֹת, שְׁלֹשָׁה אָבוֹת, שְׁנֵי לֻחוֹת הַבְּרִית, אֶחָד אֱלֹהֵינוּ שֶׁבַּשָּׁמַיִם וּבָאָרֶץ.

תִּשְׁעָה מִי יוֹדֵעַ?
תִּשְׁעָה אֲנִי יוֹדֵעַ: תִּשְׁעָה יַרְחֵי לֵידָה, שְׁמוֹנָה יְמֵי מִילָה, שִׁבְעָה יְמֵי שַׁבַּתָּא, שִׁשָּׁה סִדְרֵי מִשְׁנָה, חֲמִשָּׁה חוּמְשֵׁי תוֹרָה, אַרְבַּע אִמָּהוֹת, שְׁלֹשָׁה אָבוֹת, שְׁנֵי לֻחוֹת הַבְּרִית, אֶחָד אֱלֹהֵינוּ שֶׁבַּשָּׁמַיִם וּבָאָרֶץ.

עֲשָׂרָה מִי יוֹדֵעַ?

עֲשָׂרָה אֲנִי יוֹדֵעַ: עֲשָׂרָה דִבְּרַיָא, תִּשְׁעָה יַרְחֵי לֵידָה, שְׁ-מוֹנָה יְמֵי מִילָה, שִׁבְעָה יְמֵי שַׁבַּתָא, שִׁשָּׁה סִדְרֵי מִשְׁנָה, חֲמִשָּׁה חוּמְשֵׁי תוֹרָה, אַרְבַּע אִמָּהוֹת, שְׁלֹשָׁה אָבוֹת, שְׁנֵי לֻחוֹת הַבְּרִית אֶחָד אֱלֹהֵינוּ שֶׁבַּשָּׁמַיִם וּבָאָרֶץ.

אַחַד עָשָׂר מִי יוֹדֵעַ?

אַחַד עָשָׂר אֲנִי יוֹדֵעַ: אַחַד עָשָׂר כּוֹכְבַיָּא, עֲשָׂרָה דִבְּרַיָּא, תִּשְׁעָה יַרְחֵי לֵידָה, שְׁמוֹנָה יְמֵי מִילָה, שִׁבְעָה יְמֵי שַׁבַּתָא, שִׁשָּׁה סִדְרֵי מִשְׁנָה, חֲמִשָּׁה חוּמְשֵׁי תוֹרָה, אַרְבַּע אִמָּהוֹת, שְׁלֹשָׁה אָבוֹת, שְׁנֵי לֻחוֹת הַבְּרִית, אֶחָד אֱלֹהֵינוּ שֶׁבַּשָּׁמַיִם וּבָאָרֶץ.

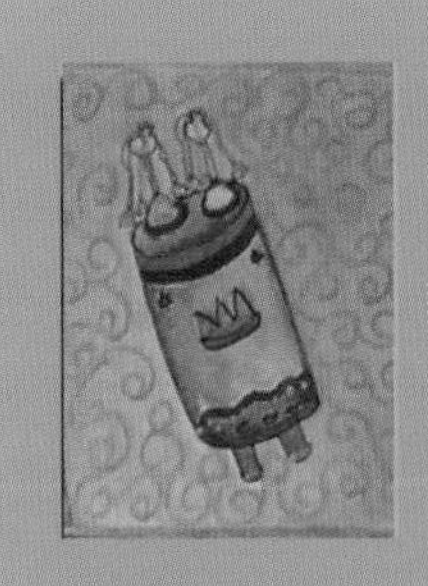

שְׁנֵים עָשָׂר מִי יוֹדֵעַ?

שְׁנֵים עָשָׂר אֲנִי יוֹדֵעַ: שְׁנֵים עָשָׂר שִׁבְטַיָּא, אַחַד עָשָׂר כּוֹכְבַיָּא, עֲשָׂרָה דִבְּרַיָּא, תִּשְׁעָה יַרְחֵי לֵידָה, שְׁמוֹנָה יְמֵי מִילָה, שִׁבְעָה יְמֵי שַׁבַּתָא, שִׁשָּׁה סִדְרֵי מִשְׁנָה, חֲמִשָּׁה חוּמְשֵׁי תוֹרָה, אַרְבַּע אִמָּהוֹת, שְׁלֹשָׁה אָבוֹת, שְׁנֵי לֻחוֹת הַבְּרִית, אֶחָד אֱלֹהֵינוּ שֶׁבַּשָּׁמַיִם וּבָאָרֶץ.

שְׁלֹשָׁה עָשָׂר מִי יוֹדֵעַ?

שְׁלֹשָׁה עָשָׂר אֲנִי יוֹדֵעַ: שְׁלֹשָׁה עָשָׂר מִדַּיָא. שְׁנֵים עָשָׂר שִׁבְטַיָּא, אַחַד עָשָׂר כּוֹכְבַיָּא, עֲשָׂרָה דִבְּרַיָּא, תִּשְׁעָה יַרְחֵי לֵידָה, שְׁמוֹנָה יְמֵי מִילָה, שִׁבְעָה יְמֵי שַׁבַּתָא, שִׁשָּׁה סִדְרֵי מִשְׁנָה, חֲמִשָּׁה חוּמְשֵׁי תוֹרָה, אַרְבַּע אִמָּהוֹת, שְׁלֹשָׁה אָבוֹת, שְׁנֵי לֻחוֹת הַבְּרִית, אֶחָד אֱלֹהֵינוּ שֶׁבַּשָּׁמַיִם וּבָאָרֶץ.

Who Knows One?

Who knows one?
I know one. One is God in heaven and on earth.

Who knows two?
I know two. Two tables of the law; One is God in heaven and on earth.

Who knows three?
I know three. Three fathers; two tables of the law;
One is God in heaven and on earth.

Who knows four?
I know four. Four mothers; three fathers; two tables of the law;
One is God in heaven and on earth.

Who knows five?
I know five. Five books of the Torah; four mothers; three fathers;
two tables of the law;
One is God in heaven and on earth.

Who knows six?
I know six. Six orders of the Mishnah; five books of the Torah;
four mothers; three fathers; two tables of the law;
One is God in heaven and on earth.

Who knows seven?
I know seven. Seven days of the week; six orders of the Mishnah;
five books of the Torah; four mothers; three fathers; two tables of the law;
One is God in heaven and on earth.

Who knows eight?

I know eight. Eight days till circumcision; seven days of the week; six orders of the Mishnah; five books of the Torah; four mothers; three fathers; two tables of the law; One is God in heaven and on earth.

Who knows nine?

I know nine. Nine months of pregnancy; eight days till circumcision; seven days of the week; six orders of the Mishnah; five books of the Torah; four mothers; three fathers; two tables of the law; One is God in heaven and on earth.

Who knows ten?

I know ten. Ten commandments; nine months of pregnancy; eight days till circumcision; seven days of the week; six orders of the Mishnah; five books of the Torah; four mothers; three fathers; two tables of the law; One is God in heaven and on earth.

Who knows eleven?

I know eleven. Eleven stars; ten commandments; nine months of pregnancy; eight days till circumcision; seven days of the week; six order of the Mishnah; five books of the Torah; four mothers; three fathers; two tables of the law; One is God in heaven and on earth.

Who knows twelve?

I know twelve. Twelve tribes; eleven stars; ten commandments; nine months of pregnancy; eight days till circumcision; seven days of the week; six orders of the Mishnah; five books of the Torah; four mothers; three fathers; two tables of the law; One is God in heaven and on earth.

Who knows thirteen?

I know thirteen. Thirteen attributes; twelve tribes; eleven stars; ten commandments; nine months of pregnancy; eight days till circumcision; seven days of the week; six orders of the Mishnah; five books of the Torah; four mothers; three fathers; two tables of the law; One is God in heaven and on earth.

Chad Gadya

This cumulative children's song, known as "Chad Gadya" in Hebrew and Aramaic, first appeared in the Passover ritual in a Haggadah printed in Prague in 1590. The melody has roots in medieval German music. This Sephardic version dates back to the nineteenth century. Versions are also available in Judeo-Italian and Judeo-Arabic.

חַד גַּדְיָא

(Hebrew/Ladino/English)

חַד גַּדְיָא, חַד גַּדְיָא, דִּזְבַן אַבָּא בִּתְרֵי זוּזֵי
חַד גַּדְיָא, חַד גַּדְיָא,
דְּזַבִּין אַבָּא בִּתְרֵי זוּזֵי

חַד גַּדְיָא, חַד גַּדְיָא
וְאָתָא שׁוּנְרָא, וְאָכְלָה לְגַדְיָא
דְּזַבִּין אַבָּא בִּתְרֵי זוּזֵי

חַד גַּדְיָא, חַד גַּדְיָא
וְאָתָא כַלְבָּא, וְנָשַׁךְ לְשׁוּנְרָא, דְּאָכְלָה לְגַדְיָא
דְּזַבִּין אַבָּא בִּתְרֵי זוּזֵי

חַד גַּדְיָא, חַד גַּדְיָא
וְאָתָא חוּטְרָא, וְהִכָּה לְכַלְבָּא
דְּנָשַׁךְ לְשׁוּנְרָא, דְּאָכְלָה לְגַדְיָא
דְּזַבִּין אַבָּא בִּתְרֵי זוּזֵי

חַד גַּדְיָא, חַד גַּדְיָא
וְאָתָא נוּרָא, וְשָׂרַף לְחוּטְרָא
דְּהִכָּה לְכַלְבָּא, דְּנָשַׁךְ לְשׁוּנְרָא,
דְּאָכְלָה לְגַדְיָא
דְּזַבִּין אַבָּא בִּתְרֵי זוּזֵי

חַד גַּדְיָא, חַד גַּדְיָא
וְאָתָא מַיָּא, וְכָבָה לְנוּרָא
דְּשָׂרַף לְחוּטְרָא, דְּהִכָּה לְכַלְבָּא
דְּנָשַׁךְ לְשׁוּנְרָא, דְּאָכְלָה לְגַדְיָא
דְּזַבִּין אַבָּא בִּתְרֵי זוּזֵי

חַד גַּדְיָא, חַד גַּדְיָא
וְאָתָא תוֹרָא, וְשָׁתָה לְמַיָּא
דְּכָבָה לְנוּרָא, דְּשָׂרַף לְחוּטְרָא
דְּהִכָּה לְכַלְבָּא, דְּנָשַׁךְ לְשׁוּנְרָא
דְּאָכְלָה לְגַדְיָא
דְּזַבִּין אַבָּא בִּתְרֵי זוּזֵי

חַד גַּדְיָא, חַד גַּדְיָא
וְאָתָא הַשּׁוֹחֵט, וְשָׁחַט לְתוֹרָא
דְּשָׁתָה לְמַיָּא, דְּכָבָה לְנוּרָא
דְּשָׂרַף לְחוּטְרָא, דְּהִכָּה לְכַלְבָּא
דְּנָשַׁךְ לְשׁוּנְרָא, דְּאָכְלָה לְגַדְיָא
דְּזַבִּין אַבָּא בִּתְרֵי זוּזֵי

חַד גַּדְיָא, חַד גַּדְיָא
וְאָתָא מַלְאַךְ הַמָּוֶת, וְשָׁחַט לְשׁוֹחֵט
דְּשָׁחַט לְתוֹרָא, דְּשָׁתָה לְמַיָּא
דְּכָבָה לְנוּרָא, דְּשָׂרַף לְחוּטְרָא
דְּהִכָּה לְכַלְבָּא, דְּנָשַׁךְ לְשׁוּנְרָא,
דְּאָכְלָה לְגַדְיָא
דְּזַבִּין אַבָּא בִּתְרֵי זוּזֵי

חַד גַּדְיָא, חַד גַּדְיָא
וְאָתָא הַקָּדוֹשׁ בָּרוּךְ הוּא
וְשָׁחַט לְמַלְאַךְ הַמָּוֶת, דְּשָׁחַט לְשׁוֹחֵט
דְּשָׁחַט לְתוֹרָא, דְּשָׁתָה לְמַיָּא
דְּכָבָה לְנוּרָא, דְּשָׂרַף לְחוּטְרָא
דְּהִכָּה לְכַלְבָּא, דְּנָשַׁךְ לְשׁוּנְרָא,
דְּאָכְלָה לְגַדְיָא
דְּזַבִּין אַבָּא בִּתְרֵי זוּזֵי
חַד גַּדְיָא, חַד גַּדְיָא

Un Cavritico

I vino el gato y se comio al cavritico
que lo merko mi padre por dos levanim por dos levanim.

I vino el perro y mordio al gato que se comio el cavritico
que lo merko mi padre por dos levanim por dos levanim.

I vino el palo y pego al perro que mordio al gato que se comio el cavritico
que lo merko mi padre por dos levanim por dos levanim.

I vino el fuego y quemo el palo que pego al perro que mordio al gato
que se comio al cavritico
que lo merko mi padre por dos levanim por dos levanim.

I vino el agua y apago el fuego que quemo al palo que pego al perro
que mordio al gato que se comio el cavritico
que lo merko mi padre por dos levanim por dos levanim.

I vino el buey y bevio el agua que apago el fuego que quemo al palo
que pego al perro que mordio al gato que se comio el cavritico
que lo merko mi padre por dos levanim por dos levanim.

I vino el shuhet y degollo al buey que bevio el agua que apago el
fuego que quemo al palo que pego al perro que mordio al gato que
se comio al cavritico
que lo merko mi padre por dos levanim por dos levanim.

I vino la muerte i mato al shuhet que degollo al buey que bevio el
agua que apago el fuego que quemo al palo que pego al perro que
mordio al gato que se comio al cavritico
que lo merko mi padre por dos levanim por dos levanim.

I vino El Santo Bindicho El, y afasto a la muerte que mato al shuhet
que degollo al buey que bevio el agua que apago el fuego que quemo
al palo que pego al perro que mordio al gato que se comio al cavritico
que lo merko mi padre por dos levanim por dos levanim.

Then came the ox
and drank the water,
that quenched the fire,
that burnt the stick,
that beat the dog,
that bit the cat,
that ate the goat,
That Father bought for two zuzim,
one little goat, one little goat.

Then came the slaughterer
and slaughtered the ox,
that drank the water,
that quenched the fire,
that burnt the stick,
that beat the dog,
that bit the cat,
that ate the goat,
That Father bought for two zuzim,
one little goat, one little goat.

Then came the Angel of Death
and killed the slaughterer,
that slaughtered the ox,
that drank the water,
that quenched the fire,
that burnt the stick,
that beat the dog,
that bit the cat,
that ate the goat,
That Father bought for two zuzim,
one little goat, one little goat.

Then came the Holy One, Blessed be He
and slew the the Angel of Death,
that killed the slaughterer,
that slaughtered the ox,
that drank the water,
that quenched the fire,
that burnt the stick,
that beat the dog,
that bit the cat,
that ate the goat,
That Father bought for two zuzim,
one little goat, one little goat.

One Little Goat

One little goat, one little goat.
That Father bought for two zuzim,
one little goat, one little goat.

Then came a cat
and ate the goat,
That Father bought for two zuzim,
one little goat, one little goat.

Then came a dog
and bit the cat,
that ate the goat,
That Father bought for two zuzim,
one little goat, one little goat.

Then came a stick
and beat the dog,
that bit the cat,
that ate the goat,
That Father bought for two zuzim,
one little goat, one little goat.

Then came fire
and burnt the stick,
that beat the dog,
that bit the cat,
that ate the goat,
That Father bought for two zuzim,
one little goat, one little goat.

Then came water
and quenched the fire,
that burnt the stick,
that beat the dog,
that bit the cat,
that ate the goat,
That Father bought for two zuzim,
one little goat, one little goat.

נִרְצָה

חֲסַל סִדּוּר פֶּסַח כְּהִלְכָתוֹ, כְּכָל מִשְׁפָּטוֹ
וְחֻקָּתוֹ. כַּאֲשֶׁר זָכִינוּ לְסַדֵּר אוֹתוֹ, כֵּן
נִזְכֶּה לַעֲשׂוֹתוֹ. זָךְ שׁוֹכֵן מְעוֹנָה, קוֹמֵם
קְהַל עֲדַת מִי מָנָה. בְּרִנָּה.

לְשָׁנָה הַבָּאָה בִּירוּשָׁלָיִם

Conclusion of the Seder

The Passover Seder is ended,
According to custom and law.
As we were worthy to celebrate it this year,
So may we celebrate it in future years.
O Holy One in Heaven above,
Restore the myriad assemblies of Israel.
Speedily lead Your redeemed people
To Zion in joy.

Next year in Jerusalem

El año próximo en Jerusalén

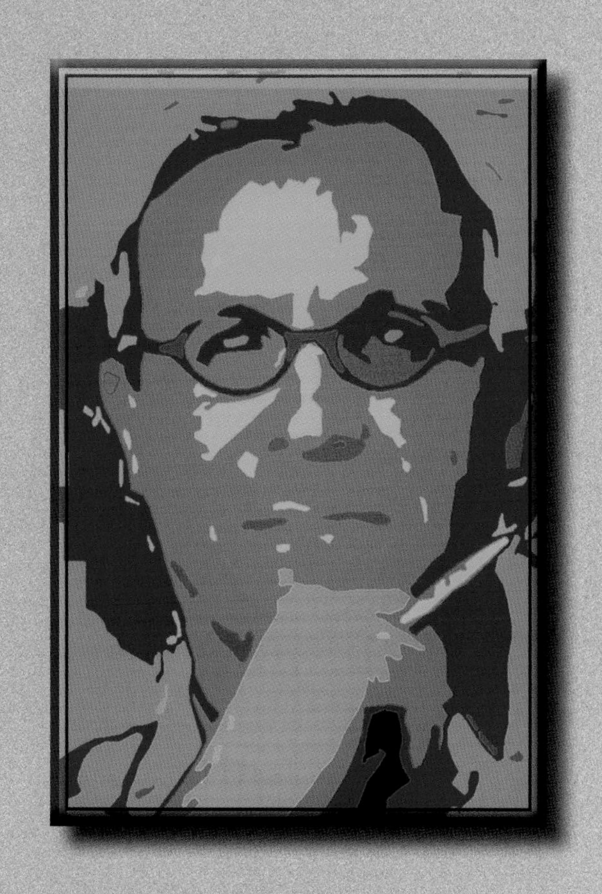

Acknowledgements

We appreciate the collaboration of David Gilad, Eliezer Nowodworski, Orit Rabkin, and Robert Sacks with Hebrew texts. The original of the poem by Rabbi Isaac Aboab da Fonseca is part of a larger manuscript in the Ets Haim Bibliotheek in Amsterdam.

Gaon Books

www.gaonbooks.com
 For permissions, group pricing, and other information contact Gaon Books, P.O. Box 23924, Santa Fe, NM 87502 or write (gaonbooks@gmail.com).

Printed in the Republic of Korea.

Library of Congress Cataloging-in-Publication Data
Stavans, Ilan, author.
The new world Haggadah / text, Ilan Stavans ; art by Gloria Abella Ballen. -- First edition. pages cm
ISBN 978-1-935604-54-9 (cloth : alk. paper) -- ISBN 978-1-935604-44-0 (pbk. : alk. paper)
1. Haggadah. 2. Haggadot--Texts. 3. Seder--Liturgy--Texts. 4. Judaism--Liturgy--Texts. I. Ballen, Gloria Abella, illustrator. II. Haggadah. III. Title.
BM674.79.S695 2015
296.4'5371--dc23
2015025997

פסח

Pesaj

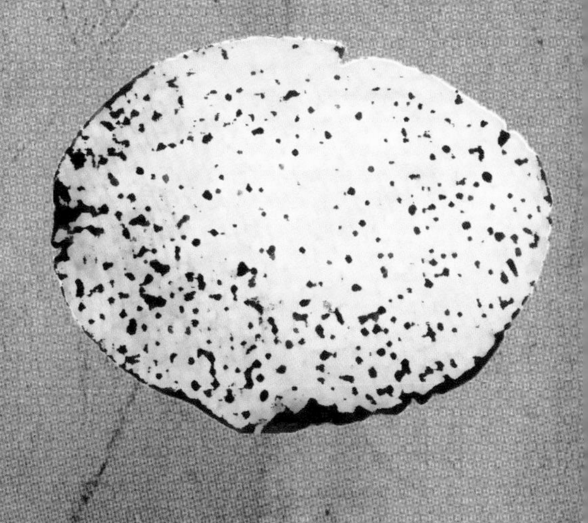